The Programming Primer:
A Guide to Programming Fundamentals

L. John Ribar

The Programming Primer:
A Guide to Programming
Fundamentals

Osborne McGraw-Hill
Berkeley New York St. Louis San Francisco Auckland Bogotá Hamburg London Madrid Mexico City
Milan Montreal New Delhi Panama City Paris São Paulo Singapore Sydney Tokyo Toronto

Osborne **McGraw-Hill**
2600 Tenth Street
Berkeley, California 94710
U.S.A.

For information on software, translations, or book distributors outside of
the U.S.A., please write to Osborne **McGraw-Hill** at the above address.

The Programming Primer: A Guide to Programming Fundamentals

1234567890 DOC 9987654

ISBN 0-07-881999-7

Series Design: Seventeenth Street Studios

This book is dedicated to Jeff Pepper, a true friend whom I've never even met.

Contents at a Glance

Contents

Acknowledgments

As always, I must acknowledge the great help from the Osborne McGraw-Hill staff, as they take a good idea and make it a good book. Thanks especially to Jeff Pepper, Nancy McLaughlin, Vicki Van Ausdall, Emily Rader, Alexa Maddox, Peter Hancik, and John Heilborn.

I also want to acknowledge an instructor I had at Westminster College in Fulton, Missouri, in my first year of formal computer science training; I vaguely remember his name as Ben Hansen. After being the head of the Computer Science department for a year, Ben went on to become a full-time concert cellist. He was one of the only programming gurus I've ever met, and I'm not sure that he even knew it. I learned more from him than what was ever taught in any class.

My greatest thanks go to my wife, Deborah, and our four children: Louis, Jamie, Michael, and Leah. Without them, completing a project like this wouldn't have a lot of meaning. Yes, kids, Daddy has finished "another book."

Introduction

Welcome to programming. Are you ready? If you fit any of the following descriptions, this book can help you:

◆ You are a manager who is in charge of one or more programmers, and you want to learn some of the buzzwords so you'll feel more at home.

◆ You have been using a computer for a while, and have heard that programming can be done in the application you are using (a spreadsheet, word processor, or database manager, most likely). You'd like to give it a try, but first you want a basic understanding of what is involved.

◆ You are a student in high school or college who wants to know more about programming before basing a whole career on it.

◆ You have heard about programming, and think you might like it as a career change. But before taking night classes, you'd like to understand what you are getting into.

◆ You are married to a programmer, or have one as a child or parent, and you want to learn more about what they do so you can spend time talking with them some time.

There may be other reasons why you want to know about programming. This book will help you learn about the programming profession and will teach you all the buzzwords, along with the concepts you will need to know in order to write programs.

Although it is assumed that you know what a computer is, where the keyboard and monitor are, and other basic skills, you do not need any knowledge of programming to read and understand this book.

What Is In This Book?

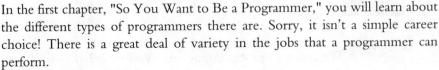

In the first chapter, "So You Want to Be a Programmer," you will learn about the different types of programmers there are. Sorry, it isn't a simple career choice! There is a great deal of variety in the jobs that a programmer can perform.

In Chapter 2, "What Is Programming?" you will learn what a program is. You will also learn how information is stored in computers, something about Boolean math, and the types of standards that exist for displaying information on your computer screen.

In Chapter 3, "Learning a New Language," you will start to learn about the kinds of information that can be managed by a computer program. You'll begin to see how learning to program is much like learning a new language. Several of the more popular languages (C, Pascal, and BASIC) will be introduced.

Chapter 4, "Using Information in Your Programs," shows how the types of information described in Chapter 3 are actually used in computer programs. Because you are not yet using a language for programming, the examples are shown in three languages (again, C, Pascal, and BASIC) to more fully explain the concepts presented, and to give you a feel for how these languages look and work in practice.

In Chapter 5, "Controlling the Flow," you will learn about managing the order in which things happen in a program. You will learn about incorporating decisions into your programs, looping, program blocks, and the infamous **GOTO** statement.

Chapter 6, "Programming in Pieces," focuses on program design techniques. These techniques become increasingly important as you begin to write larger programs. This chapter also describes the process of breaking a program down into smaller, easily understandable pieces. Libraries, APIs, and multifile projects are also discussed.

To give you some hands-on experience using the information you have learned in the first six chapters, Chapter 7, "Pulling It All Together," assigns you a program that needs to be written. You are led through the design of a check-printing program, and then into the programming process itself. Solutions written in C, Pascal, and BASIC round out the chapter.

In Chapter 8, "New Development Technologies," you are introduced to some of the latest programming tools, including computer-aided software engineering (CASE) and object-oriented programming systems (OOPs). You will read about graphical user interfaces (GUIs) and event-driven programming, and learn what to look for in a development environment.

The four appendices are more than just reference material; they present information designed to complement the earlier sections of the book and expand your ability to grow as a programmer. Appendix A, "ASCII and EBCDIC Characters, and Their Corresponding Numeric Values," shows the differences between the two most common character sets currently in use with computer systems. Appendix B, "A Programming Glossary," provides definitions for many of the terms used in this book, along with a few others that will help round out your programming vocabulary. Appendix C, "Programming Languages and Compilers—A List of Vendors," lists some of the more common programming systems available, and offers information on how to find them. Finally, Appendix D, "Where to Find Out More," lists some books and magazines, along with personal recommendations, that can help you evolve as a programmer.

For Your Enjoyment

Throughout the book, there are several quotations from *The Tao of Programming,* by Geoffrey James. This book, published in 1987 by Info Books, is a jewel for any programmer's bookshelf, and is one of the few computer books left that is priced under ten dollars! You can write to Info Books at P.O. Box 1018, Santa Monica, CA 90406.

Conventions

This book has only a few conventions. If you see something in bold, like **IF...THEN** or **WHILE**, you'll know it is something you will actually see in a program.

If you see something in italics, *like this,* you'll know it is a definition that you might want to learn. Many of these definitions appear in Computer Lingo boxes. Taking the time to learn these definitions will help improve your ability to speak with other programmers.

Write Home

 As you learn more, and make decisions about programming, feel free to send the author your stories. You can write to me at the following address:

L. John Ribar, CCP
Picasso Software Group Ltd.
CYBER Center
1600 Pennsylvania Avenue
York, PA 17404

In the process, you might also find about a great company that does training, consulting, and custom application design.

Now is the time. Let's learn about programming!

Chapter 1

So You Want to Be a

Programmer

1

PROGRAMMING can be a most rewarding pastime. Programming can also be mundane and painstaking. Since it is a professional occupation, there is a certain amount of training required to become a programmer, and a number of designations that can be achieved. But there is also a good deal of artistry involved, at least if you want to move to the higher echelons of the industry.

In this first chapter, you'll learn a little about the software profession. This includes some possible reasons for becoming involved in programming, the types of programming that are available, and the stages of progress in a programmer's evolution.

Money, Prestige, and Glory

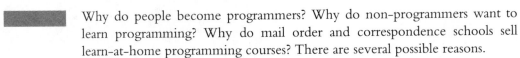

Why do people become programmers? Why do non-programmers want to learn programming? Why do mail order and correspondence schools sell learn-at-home programming courses? There are several possible reasons.

♦ **Fame and Fortune?**   Most programmers are not rich, and you probably cannot name more than a few famous programmers (if any) unless you are really into the industry. Programming has many levels of pay—from just above the poverty level up to six figures or more, based on the type of work you do and the experience you have. (You will learn more about various types of programming in the next section of this chapter.) Fame and fortune are certainly valid goals, but be prepared to work hard to achieve them.

♦ **Control?**   This is possibly a better reason. Although it may not be immediately apparent, learning to program gives you the ultimate control over your computer. In fact, a computer is more obedient than a dog—once you teach it a trick, it always performs the same way!

◆ **It's Just a Job?** Many of the advertisements for learn-at-home programming courses will have you think that all it takes is "a few short weeks, and you too can be a programmer, earning the respect of your friends, the admiration of your spouse, and new levels of pay that you never thought existed." Before you jump, look at the next section of this chapter, where you learn about the different levels of programming. You *can* learn programming quickly, but to be really good takes time and talent, and it's the really good people who make the money.

◆ **It Just Feels Right?** This is possibly the best reason for being a programmer, whether as a full-time job, as an enhancement to your regular job, or as a hobby. When you start learning more about programming, you will probably fall into one of two categories: either it feels right, or it feels wrong. If it feels right, you should learn to program at some level, just for the satisfaction it can bring into your life. If it feels wrong, you should probably look into something else. This is not to say that you cannot be a programmer; many people have become programmers when it felt "wrong," but doing it this way requires much more work and discipline.

note:

It is interesting that many younger people are now getting into programming in order to write game programs. There are a great many games available on electronic bulletin boards and elsewhere that are written by young teenagers. Using the imagination and learning capabilities that they still have as younger folks, they often produce some of the very best programs available. They are, however, usually limited to game programs, probably because of their interest level. A primary goal in the world of professional programming should be to train these talented minds in the development process and apply their skills to the needs of the business world. At least the results might make our everyday work on computers more fun!

Your reason for programming may be one of those listed above, or may be something totally different. In any case, the next sections will detail your possibilities in programming.

Enhancing Your Normal (Non-Programming) Job

It used to be true that you could go through an entire career and never have to learn anything about computers. It wasn't that long ago that computers had no place in the workplace.

But recent changes in almost every type of work have brought computers in touch with people at nearly all levels, and the pace is quickening.

◆   Cashiers at fast-food restaurants use computer-based terminals as cash registers. While these do the work expected of the old, manual cash registers (totalling the order, collecting money, providing change), they also collect data for daily sales reports, determine inventory ordering requirements, pass instructions to the cooks, and communicate with the company's host computer, allowing an overall look at buying trends and sales figures for a single store or an entire chain. Naturally, all this is happening in the background, while you hungrily eat your ration of fast food.

◆   Clerks in retail stores use similar computerized cash registers. These perform many of the same functions as in the fast food industry, but also keep an eye on trends—what stays in fashion, and what quietly fades into the past. This data helps retail buyers determine the types of inventory that should be carried.

◆   To deliver inventory to the retail industries, most trucking companies have turned to computers for planning. Determination of the best routes, combinations of deliveries to reduce the time and distance involved (thus reducing cost), and selection of the least expensive of multiple trucking companies are all handled by computer. In many cases, the actual delivery information, billing, and payments are all handled electronically, via computers tied to the phone lines.

◆   To provide the best mix of inventory for shipping, most warehouses and distribution centers have moved to computers. A forklift operator is now told, via a radio transmission to his or her own tiny computer (on the forklift!), what items need to be selected and brought to the trucks for shipping. The computer indicates where the items can be found, and consistently make selections aimed at getting the right products out before they become outdated. In addition, storage of inventory is managed by computer so that warehouse space can be efficiently utilized.

◆   To provide the goods to fill the warehouses, factories and manufacturing facilities of all types are becoming more dependent on computers. Everything from cookies to cars are now produced under fully auto-mated processes, controlled mostly or even entirely by computer.

◆   The banking industry is totally dependent on computers. All transactions and balances are computerized. The 24-hour tellers now located almost everywhere are all small computers, tied into networks of computers that allow the passing of account information on a quick, automated basis.

◆ Professionals, such as doctors, dentists, veterinarians, accountants, and hairdressers, are using computers more and more to maintain customer records and manage billings. This makes it simple, for instance, to send out a special advertisement to people who haven't been in for six months (in the case of a dentist), or who haven't been in for a perm in eight weeks (for a hairdresser), or who haven't paid their bill in two months (useful for everyone!). Many in the medical and dental professions can even tie their computers directly to their patients' insurance companies, thus speeding the processing of claims and reducing overall costs for everyone involved.

◆ The construction, contracting, and engineering professions now use computers to design and draw the things that are being built. Often, the same software that designs a project will produce estimates for the cost of its construction, based on the drawings. Some programs will even produce a list of the parts needed, an estimate of manpower requirements, and an estimated time of completion.

◆ Authors are turning more and more to computers for their writing. This book, and most others currently being written, was written entirely on a computer, and transmitted electronically to the publisher's computer, where notes were made directly on the computer and passed back for my revisions. This saves a great deal of time and money, not to mention the trees saved by not printing out multiple copies of each chapter, and the cost saving of not sending bulky documents through the mail or express systems.

What does this all mean to you as a programmer? All of these uses for computers, and all those that have yet to be discovered, require programming. Whatever your interests, there can be a way to apply programming skills.

People in many professions have become their own secretaries and accountants, through the use of personal computers and amazing software creations. Word processors automate the typing of letters, reports, and the like. Spreadsheet software allows all kinds of manipulation of numeric data, enhanced by graphic representations that rival those produced professionally. Presentation software helps the average computer user create the kind of overheads and handouts that used to require an art department.

Many of these software packages now include programming utilities, allowing the user to automate routine tasks. For instance, a spreadsheet can contain "programming" that asks you a few questions, and then performs a myriad of calculations, presenting you with a graphical answer at the end. Word processors can be "programmed" to format paragraphs in a certain way, based on the commands that you give. While this is not the type of programming that takes four years of college to learn, it is programming nonetheless, and what you learn throughout this book will help you in these tasks.

Beyond the programmability offered by these products, someone has to actually write the entire programs in the first place. This is where programming becomes a full-time job.

It's Just a Job

Programming as a profession can be very exciting, can simply pay the bills, or can be a real pain in the neck. Sometimes you can experience all of these feelings while working for a single employer, depending on the current project or function to which you are assigned.

There are several levels of computers on which you can program. *Mainframe computers* are large, expensive, multiuser computers used in many accounting and material resource planning (MRP) operations for large companies. Often, there will also be a large staff of programmers who write small *utilities,* or small programs, that add functionality to the main processing of the system (an extra report for the accounting program, a special billing run, etc.).

Another level of programming involves creating utilities for minicomputers and microcomputers, referred to in this book as PCs (for Personal Computers). In these types of jobs, you can look forward to a great multitude of assignments, depending on the company you work for and the tasks that need to be accomplished. One company might have you in charge of the printing function for a word processor. Another might ask that you produce utility programs for their database manager.

note: *Historically, minicomputers and microcomputers have served two different markets, with minicomputers used by small and medium groups of people, and microcomputers working for a single user at a time. Due to the rapid growth of computer hardware capabilities in microcomputers, the distinction is nearly gone. Many of the software programs and operating systems that once were only available on minicomputers are now sold for microcomputers, so the two will be treated together in this book.*

A small company might have you programming an entire application. If you approach this type of work as "just a job," you may experience rapid burnout; smaller companies typically place more responsibility on each programmer than do larger companies, and the number of hours required can increase rapidly.

Computer Lingo

When you do the same thing for too long, at too great an intensity, the fatigue, irritability, and general bad health that can result is known as *burnout*. For instance, working an occasional 80-hour week may be no problem, but if you have to do it for weeks or months on end, it may create havoc in your life.

Personal Satisfaction (or...It's an Addiction!)

If you really enjoy programming, however, it may become more than just a job to you; it might become an addiction. For many people, programming is a purely enjoyable way to spend time. For someone addicted to programming, there is little that can compare with the joy of successfully completing a programming project. The number of programmers who have "regular" jobs, but who prefer programming as a hobby, is growing steadily. Much of the reason for this is the increasing availability of programming environments that allow even beginning programmers to produce useful programs. In later chapters of this book, you'll see some of these environments.

note: *Burnout is possible for home programming addicts, just like it is for overworked professional programmers, if too many projects are attempted at the same time. If you have a 40-hour per week job, and spend four or five hours a night programming, you can quickly burn yourself out, and then both your job and your hobby (as well as your family and other important things in your life) are liable to suffer. To prevent this, make sure that you spend time on other projects and activities, or schedule regular days when you don't program. (This may be hard to imagine, but it is possible.) Amazingly, as you work on other things, you might find yourself thinking about how your other tasks could be assisted with a good program! Also, as you take a break from your current programming project, you allow your mind the chance to work on other problems that might have been bothering you, programming or otherwise.*

In the early days of computing, programmers who spent all their free time programming were called *hackers*. Many of them would rather hack around with a computer, finding out what could and could not be done, than anything else. This is where many of the early programming ideas came from—programmers working late at night and on weekends, producing what would become software for the rest of us, trying all different possibilities until something worked.

Unfortunately, in the last few years the term "hacker" has taken on a sinister meaning, with much bad press revolving around people who wanted to find out how systems worked so they could *break* them, or *break into* them. Many of the other terms used to describe intense computer users are not quite complimentary either: computer weenies, computer nerds, computer junkies, chip heads, etc.

Nevertheless, much of the best software is still produced by programmers working at home. The problem is that software has become such a big business that even excellent programs generally don't do well without the backing of a large company. Advertising, marketing, and support costs can kill the budgets of smaller companies.

There is still hope, however, for individual programmers and small firms. One method of distribution, called *shareware,* allows you to distribute your newest software creation worldwide within hours through electronic networks (called Bulletin Board Systems, or BBSs). As people try the software, they either pay you for your work, or stop using the program. For many who only have their home budgets from which to finance software purchases, the shareware concept has great merit. You can try the software at no charge. In fact, you can try as many programs of the same type as you want. When you pick one that you like, you only pay for that one.

Most people don't get rich producing shareware, but if you develop a good program, shareware can get it out to a lot of people in a short time. Once you've established a base of satisfied users, you can approach the magazines and bigger companies to seek publicity and financial backing. By this time your program will be well-tested, and most of the bugs will already be worked out.

Computer Lingo

ugs are parts of a computer program that do not work as expected. The name *bugs* historically comes from a hardware failure in an early Univac system, the size of a ballroom, that was caused by a small moth that had found its way into the computer. Another term used commonly is *software defects*.

Now that we've explored some of the situations that might result once you learn how to program, let's review some of the stages you might go through as you become a programmer.

Stages of a Programmer's Evolution

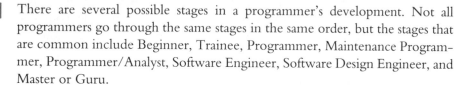 There are several possible stages in a programmer's development. Not all programmers go through the same stages in the same order, but the stages that are common include Beginner, Trainee, Programmer, Maintenance Programmer, Programmer/Analyst, Software Engineer, Software Design Engineer, and Master or Guru.

Beginner or Trainee

Many professions use the terms "beginner" and "trainee" to designate people who haven't really learned the ropes yet. You probably won't hear these terms used in the programming profession. However, if you are learning to program, you need to consider yourself a beginner just to keep yourself safe.

If you are training in a new job to answer telephones, and you do it wrong, you may miss some calls, and some people might even have to call back. If you write software to control automated machinery in a factory and something goes wrong, you might be liable for thousands of dollars of damage, and even the loss of life. Of course, not everyone does this type of programming, but when you first learn to program, don't try to take on the world all at once.

Beginning programming is a "try it until you succeed or fail" proposition. You need to play around with programming to learn it, and while you are learning, you need to make mistakes so that you see how things work. The best types of programs for beginners are small utilities, little programs that help you in your own work. When you write these little gems, you have the perfect opportunity to test your finished programs—in your own work! Also, since you write them for yourself, no one gets hurt if they don't work. If you don't like the way they work, you can improve them yourself.

Probably the most important thing to learn as a beginning programmer is that you need to try new things until you become comfortable with them. This means that you may spend a lot of personal time until you become proficient; most bosses won't let you sit around playing all day. But if you don't get your hands dirty, you will probably never learn programming.

Very often, the beginning phase of a programmer's development will be spent in a school setting (college, technical school, or training classes provided by your employer). In fact, more and more young people these days are starting to program at home, while they are in high school, junior high, and even elementary school.

The trainee phase usually starts when you get your first programming job, or when you are first assigned a programming task to supplement your normal job. This is actually the early part of the programmer phase. Having small programming tasks to complete helps you build your confidence, and the confidence of your employer, without any real risk should you have problems along the way.

Programmer

After a training period, when you perform small tasks with little risk, you will move into the ranks of true programmers. Now you will receive larger pieces of programs to complete. Very often, you will work with a team of programmers on a large project or a portion of a project.

The most effective programming teams are generally in the range of two to eight people, and more than one of these teams may cooperate to build large systems. For instance, in the defense industry, it is not uncommon to have several hundred programmers working on a single project. A project of this size will usually be organized and maintained by a full-time programming manager.

Many of today's PC applications were originally developed by only one or two people. Once a program was accepted by the public, and sales started rolling in, additional programmers were usually added to the team to add functionality, create demonstration programs, and develop add-on utilities aimed at producing a more marketable program.

As a programmer, you will probably be following the overall design set forth by someone else (a Programmer/Analyst or Software Engineer), creating only the portions of the program that are assigned to you. Of course, if you are working for yourself, or programming at home, your program will follow your own design.

Maintenance Programmer

Once a program is written, someone is generally assigned the job of Maintenance Programmer. This type of work is usually thought of as being less fun, because someone else has already written the program. Fortunately, maintenance programming can be very rewarding as a learning experience.

Maintenance programming involves the support and improvement of programs that have been developed by someone else. This means that you have to first learn the program and understand what the original programmer wanted to do in all the portions of the program. Then, as bugs arise, or improvements are suggested, you need to determine where and how the necessary changes should be made.

This type of programming thus becomes a blend of psychology (figuring out what the original programmer was doing), exploration and discovery (locating areas where improvements can be made), detective work (finding the bugs), and investigative reporting (determining whether the changes you *might* make will affect any other parts of the program).

Programmer/Analyst

Once you have been programming for a while, you may become a Programmer/Analyst. While this promotion often requires some additional training, it allows you to become a more integral part of the design process.

An analyst's primary task is to analyze the problem that needs to be solved. This process will usually involve interviewing the users or potential users of the program to find out what changes, if any, need to be made. You must then determine whether the changes should be *procedural* (affecting how the program is used) or *systematic* (affecting how the program works).

note:

There are two types of problems you must solve for your users: procedural and systematic. Suppose that you work for an accounting firm, and you propose using a spreadsheet program to track financial data. The spreadsheet software you've selected has all the right features to manage this task; the systematic part of the solution is therefore complete. However, the procedural problem still needs to be solved: Yes, the program will do everything the firm requires, but how will they use it? What procedures will they need to follow? Do they know which type of spreadsheet to use, and where in the spreadsheet to make entries? Do they know about sharing files and making backups? These are all procedural questions, and the answers you come up with will be important elements of the final solution you provide.

Once you have thoroughly analyzed the problem at hand, you will write up a report summarizing the problem and proposing a new program or program feature that should fix it. Then you will present the report to the users (and your boss), and wait for their decision.

This can often be the most prolonged part of programming—users are not well-known for making firm decisions about their needs and desires, especially if there is a time or money budget. Usually, decisions must be made regarding which features can be produced while still maintaining a fixed budget. Another problem is that there are usually several users for each program and, as in many group situations, gaining a consensus is not always easy. This is an important reason to get everything in writing!

Finally a decision will be made, and you, as the Programmer/Analyst, will be called upon to make the changes or to head the team who will make the changes.

Computer Lingo

Users of computer programs are no different than other consumers—they want their program to do everything, but they only want to pay what they want to pay. Often, once an agreement is made, you will have the task of holding back *creeping elegance*. Creeping elegance is what happens when users think of new features that they would like to have in their programs, but for which there is no budget. You should generally avoid trying to accommodate such late-breaking user requests; otherwise, you'll end up blowing your own budget trying to complete the project. One way of trying to prevent this problem is to ask detailed questions during the analysis stage, encouraging the users to think carefully, long before the budget is finalized, about what there exact needs are.

Software Engineer and Software Design Engineer

A Software Engineer can have many different titles (each company seems to have its own), including Software Design Engineer, System Design Engineer, Computer Scientist, or Software Designer. Most of these titles will have similar functions.

A Software Engineer is a step up the ladder from the Programmer/Analyst. The Software Engineer becomes more involved in the design process, and in how the process *itself* works. This process, commonly referred to as the software development methodology, is discussed more fully in Chapter 6.

Most Software Engineers have college degrees, as well as a good deal of experience in the development of software. And while they work more with the design process, they are still very much a part of the development process, and can continue to program if they desire. In some larger software firms, the Software Engineers may construct a design for the overall program and then head a team of programmers, who will program the actual code that completes the design.

Master or Guru

This is a level of programming not reached by many people in their programming careers. Programming gurus (also known as software masters) are those who have enough training, experience, and talent that they can solve virtually any programming problem.

Very often, a software master starts life as a hacker, playing at programming until he or she understands how programming works from the inside. Then, solving software problems becomes a simple task of manipulating the elements until they work together correctly.

You will probably have a guru where you work. Most companies have an appointed guru, or someone who fits the description more than anyone else on staff. This is the person you go to when you have problems with your programming tasks.

A real software guru, however, may not work in this type of environment. Real gurus have the software process embedded internally. They know when the software *feels* right. How the process should work is part of them; there is no need for looking up diagrams in books. Design work is often done in their heads, and many gurus can actually think through several trains of thought at once.

note:

Many large corporations create special positions for people who are at the guru level, or who show unique creative promise. Usually these people are given a job, for a year or three, where all they do is...be creative. This might involve sitting back with their feet up, thinking of the next great solution; it might involve trying out new programming ideas. You may not get rich or famous as a guru, but there are often special perks that you can receive, and this type of job is one of them.

If you meet a software master, learn all you can. Listen and watch how the guru works, and figure out how to apply what you learn to your own programming. This may be the best training you'll ever find.

At the Starting Gate . . .

 You probably now know all that you ever wanted to know about the programming profession. In the chapters that follow, you will learn what it takes to actually start programming. We'll begin by discussing what a computer program is, and why programs are necessary.

Chapter 2

What Is Programming?

EFORE you start learning about programming, you should have a firm understanding of what it entails—and what it does not entail. In this chapter, you will learn about what a program is, what types of information can be used in programs, and how the computer handles this information. As part of this discussion, we will examine different numbering systems (binary, decimal, and hexadecimal) and their significance in computer programming, as well as the functions that let you get information into and out of your programs.

What Is a Program?

A program is a sequence of instructions for a computer. This can be as simple as a DOS BATch file or a Lotus 1-2-3 macro, or as complex as a spreadsheet program written in C or assembly language. (You'll learn more about these languages in the next chapter.) Why do programs need to be written?

Computers, no matter how you look at them, are really just big machines. They are no smarter than your toaster, no more flexible than your lawnmower— that is, until you add a program. The program is what makes the computer *seem* smart. In reality, the computer is not any smarter than it was without the program; it is just doing what the programmer has told it to do in certain situations. However, to someone who does not know better, the computer may look very intelligent. In fact, if the programmer is very smart, or very clever, the computer can act as if it had a mind of its own.

But the computer is still a machine. A popular saying with computers is "Garbage In, Garbage Out." This is how a computer works: if you put garbage in (faulty programs and inaccurate or missing data), you will get garbage out (unexpected responses, erroneous results, or no answers at all). On the other hand, if you enter well-designed programs into the computer, and fill them with sound data, you will find the computer to be an amazing tool that can help in almost any aspect of life (or at least your job).

When your bank makes a mistake on your statement, it is not the computer's fault, no matter how many times the bank clerks may tell you that! Either someone has entered the information incorrectly, or the program that runs on the bank's computer contains an error which has not been found or corrected by the programmer. The computer only does what it is told, and *exactly* what it is told! So being a programmer, you have a great responsibility to tell the computer exactly what you want done.

A program, then, is a sequence of commands that you give the computer, telling it what to display, what questions to ask, where to get its information, what calculations to perform, and what to do with the results. Programs are written in programming *languages,* which are similar to the many languages we speak, except that computer languages are specifically designed for communicating with computers.

Some of the more common programming languages have names like C, C++, Pascal, Modula-2, ADA, PL/I, FORTRAN, COBOL, Lisp, Smalltalk, and BASIC. But there are also languages built into some of the programs that you may currently use: DOS BATCH, Lotus 1-2-3 macros, LotusScript, Microsoft WordBasic, and many more. Also, many database programs have their own programming languages, usually called xBASE (based on the dBASE product from Borland), or SQL (pronounced "sequel"), which is an abbreviation for Structured Query Language.

How do you tell the computer what to do? You use one of the programming languages to write specific instructions—your program. Then you give what you've written to a special computer program, called a *compiler,* which converts your program into something the computer can understand.

Why can't the computer use your original, uncompiled program? In fact, why doesn't the computer understand plain English? The following discussion will help to answer these questions, and help to build your background knowledge of how computers work on the inside.

Without information, there would be little use for computers or programming. With the exception of computer games, almost all programs deal with information of some sort. Actually, even game programs use information: You are given background information, or the current status of the game, which you use to make certain decisions. Your responses are the information that is fed back into the computer, allowing the game to continue, and determining its course of events.

No matter what type of program is being used, all information is ultimately stored in the computer as a series of *bits.* A bit is the smallest piece of information in a computer; each bit can have the value 0 or 1. *Bytes* and *nibbles* are collections of bits; a nibble is four bits, and a byte is eight bits, as Figure 2-1 illustrates.

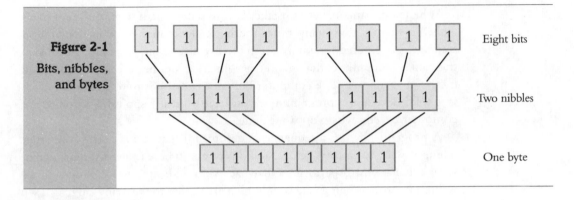

Figure 2-1

Bits, nibbles, and bytes

Eight bits

Two nibbles

One byte

Computer Lingo

The word *bit* comes from *binary digit*. Since computers use binary numbers in their fundamental operations, each bit represents one of the binary digits (0 or 1).

The computer uses the binary numbering system to store and manipulate all information, including the actual programs that run on the computer. Binary numbers look like sequences of the digits 0 and 1 (which is where bits get their values). This system will probably seem odd, since humans generally use decimal numbers (base 10, that is). To understand why computers function in binary, you should know how numbering systems work. This basic knowledge is important for anyone who wants to become an effective programmer.

Numbering Systems

What is the binary numbering system, and how does it work? How is it different from the decimal system, which you use every day? What are the hexadecimal (or hex) and octal numbering systems? Knowing the answers to these questions will help you to better understand the inner workings of the computer.

Why Binary?

The light switches in your home have only two possible settings: on and off. A computer is really only a machine with millions of on-off switches. It was a

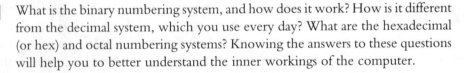

natural decision to use the binary numbering system for computers. Each binary digit has only two values: 0, which is used to represent a switch being turned off, and 1, which represents the switch being on. Within the computer, the CPU (Central Processing Unit), or the brain of the machine, can only do work with two values: 0 and 1. These values represent the two possible states of each switch. Internally, then, all information in the computer is stored as a series of on and off values, or 1's and 0's.

note:

There are indeed millions of switches inside the small computer on your desk. The switches are embedded in the silicon chip inside the computer. Technology has found a way, through the use of semiconductor materials, to miniaturize the switches to the point where millions can fit in an area about the size of a postage stamp.

WHAT ARE BINARY NUMBERS?

The most commonly used numbering system is the decimal system. There are ten possible digits in this system:

0
1
2
3
4
5
6
7
8
9

Decimal numbers are also known as a *base 10* numbers. Binary numbers, on the other hand, are *base 2* numbers. Therefore, the only digits that can be used are 0 and 1. But how are these numbers formed?

The following table summarizes the values for several of the standard bases used in computing, and how they correspond with the decimal numbering system.

You can use this table to calculate the value of the hex number 123, as shown in Figure 2-2.

Base	Fourth Column	Third Column	Second Column	First Column
Hexadecimal	16	$16 \times 16 \times 16$	16×16	16	1
Decimal	10	$10 \times 10 \times 10$	10×10	10	1
Octal	8	$8 \times 8 \times 8$	8×8	8	1
Binary	2	$2 \times 2 \times 2$	2×2	2	1

WHAT ARE OCTAL AND HEX NUMBERS

For simplicity, many computer books, as well as programmers, will use the hexadecimal (base 16) or octal (base 8) numbering system. These systems work very well for representing binary numbers, because eight and sixteen are powers of 2. Therefore, each octal digit represents three binary digits ($2 \times 2 \times 2 = 8$), and each hex digit represents four binary digits ($2 \times 2 \times 2 \times 2 = 16$). Figure 2-3 shows how these numbers are related.

Octal numbers only allow the digits 0 through 7, and binary numbers only use 0 and 1. The hexadecimal system, however, is base 16. Therefore, the ten digits you normally use for decimal numbers are not enough. For hex numbers, the letters A through F are used to represent the additional six digits, with the following values:

Hex Value	Decimal Value
0	0
1	1
2	2
3	3
4	4
5	5
6	6
7	7
8	8
9	9
A	10
B	11
C	12
D	13
E	14
F	15
10	16

Figure 2-2

Calculating the value of 123 hex

```
123 Hex  =  1   2   3
                     |
                     | 3 x 1      =   3
                 | 2 x 16      =  32
             1 x 16 x 16       = 256
                                ─────
                               291  Decimal
```

Character Sets

Using the binary numbering system, only two characters (0 and 1) can be represented. For this reason, computers are designed to use eight bits together (one byte) to produce each individual character. In this way 256 unique codes, or 256 characters, can be represented. (In computer programming, as in basic handwriting, *characters* are simply the individual letters and symbols that combine to form the words, numeric expressions, and other terms that you use.)

Certain standards have been set up to determine the numbers that will be stored for each character. These standards, known as *character sets,* describe not only the numbers that are used to represent each character, but also what characters can be used on the computer system. For instance, some character sets only allow uppercase letters, while others support both uppercase and lowercase letters.

There are multiple standards to choose from. The most common in use today is the ASCII (American Standard Code for Information Interchange) standard, which consists of 128 standard codes and 128 extended codes. The standard codes are available on all ASCII-based computers. The characters they represent

Figure 2-3

Corresponding binary, octal, and hex numbers

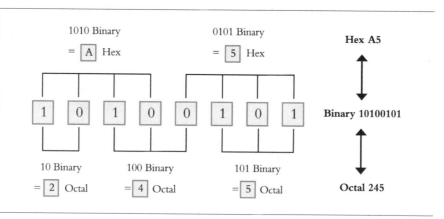

include all those found on a standard English typewriter, along with a number of special characters and graphic symbols. The extended codes are only available on the IBM-compatible personal computers. They represent an assortment of non-English characters, line-drawing characters, and additional symbols.

Does it matter which standard you select? In the next section, you'll see why the answer to this question is a definitive "yes."

Why Standards Are Important

There is definitely a good reason to be sure that you pick the right standard. If you were to pick one character set, and your associates picked another, you would not be able to exchange data! Why?

The computer stores each character as a number, based on the standard you select. However, the letter "A" in the ASCII standard has the value 65, while the EBCDIC standard uses 193 for the same letter. Since computers only understand numbers, your computer would see the 193 from your friend as something much different than the letter "A."

Don't worry too much about character sets, though. While there are different standards in existence, they are fixed in regard to the audiences they serve. For instance, ASCII is universally accepted on personal computers and on most minicomputers. EBCDIC is more widely accepted on larger computers.

If you plan to stay with a single type of computer (PCs, for example), you may never even come in contact with the character set standards used by other types. But if you start working with computers of different manufacture and size, be sure to find out whether data will need translation as it flows from one system to the other.

Common ASCII and EBCDIC Values

Table 2-1 shows some common characters, along with their related values in the ASCII and EBCDIC standards. A complete table of these values is shown in Appendix A.

Most of the information you'll want to store will probably not be in single characters (or in binary numbers). Undoubtedly, you will also use real numbers, integers, and strings of characters (names, addresses, etc.). In the sections that follow, you'll learn more about how these different types of data are classified and processed by the computer.

Character	ASCII Value	EBCDIC Value	Character	ASCII Value	EBCDIC Value
A	65	193	a	97	129
B	66	194	b	98	130
C	67	195	c	99	131
D	68	196	d	100	132
E	69	197	e	101	133
F	70	198	f	102	134
G	71	199	g	103	135
H	72	200	h	104	136
I	73	201	i	105	137
J	74	209	j	106	145
K	75	210	k	107	146
L	76	211	l	108	147
M	77	212	m	109	148
N	78	213	n	110	149
O	79	214	o	111	150
P	8	215	p	112	151
Q	81	216	q	113	152
R	82	217	r	114	153
S	83	226	s	115	162
T	84	227	t	116	163
U	85	228	u	117	164
V	86	229	v	118	165
W	87	230	w	119	166
X	88	231	x	120	167
Y	89	232	y	121	168
Z	90	233	z	122	169
0	48	240	!	33	90
1	49	241	#	35	123
2	50	242	$	36	91
3	51	243	%	37	108
4	52	244	&	38	80
5	53	245	(	40	77
6	54	246	)	41	93
7	55	247	*	42	92
8	56	248	?	63	111
9	57	249	(space)	32	64

Table 2-1
Common ASCII and EBCDIC values

note: 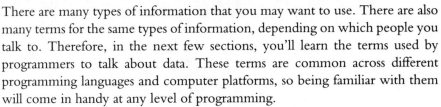 *There are other character sets besides ASCII and EBCDIC. These include Baudot, Transcode, and other versions of the ASCII standard. However, these sets are not commonly used. In fact, for PCs and most minicomputers, you will probably only use the ASCII characters, while for mainframe computers, the EBCDIC set is more common.*

Data Types

There are many types of information that you may want to use. There are also many terms for the same types of information, depending on which people you talk to. Therefore, in the next few sections, you'll learn the terms used by programmers to talk about data. These terms are common across different programming languages and computer platforms, so being familiar with them will come in handy at any level of programming.

The major data types that are common across all systems are *integers*; *floating point* (or *real*) *numbers*; *characters* and *strings*; and *Boolean* (or *logical*) *values*.

Integers

Integers are counting numbers. These are the numbers you learned in kindergarten and first grade:

1 2 3 4 5 6 7 8 9 10 11 12 . . .

but they also include the number zero, and the negative numbers. The complete set therefore includes:

. . . –5 –4 –3 –2 –1 0 1 2 3 4 5 . . .

The basic thing that sets integers apart from other sets of numbers is that there are only whole numbers, no portions of numbers. If you need to count or total whole numbers, integers are the data type you will use.

Some languages will allow you to have special integers that have only positive or zero values, without any negatives. These types may be called *unsigned integers* or *cardinal numbers*.

Some languages also allow the specification of the size of the integer, that is, how large an integer may be stored in a computer storage location. While this will be discussed in more detail in Chapter 4, suffice it to say that the terms *long integer* and *short integer* are often used to specify that a larger or smaller number can be stored.

Floating Point (Real) Numbers

Floating point numbers are often called real numbers. Real numbers include all the integers, and all the fractional numbers used in mathematical calculations. These numbers are very important. Can you imagine the bank calculating your interest without being able to use real numbers? The 3.4% interest on your savings would drop to 3%, and the 11.7% interest on your car loan would become 12%.

Some programming languages also allow the specification of the size of floating point numbers. As you will see in Chapter 4, the words *long, short,* and *double* are often used with real numbers to specify that a program will allow a larger or smaller number to be stored.

Characters

Characters are the letters that you use to write names, addresses, instructions, questions, and other textual items. These are the letters of the alphabet, plus numbers, and all special symbols.

Since most of the words you use are longer than a single character, most programming languages will have a data type known as a *string*.

Strings

Strings are sequences of characters used in words and sentences. Most programming languages provide a method for handling strings. If the computer were not able to *string* characters together into longer units, a lot of time would be spent trying to process information character by character.

Boolean (Logical) Values

Boolean data has two values: TRUE and FALSE. Boolean data is also known as *logical data.* This is an ideal data type for a computer because the values TRUE and FALSE are easily represented by on and off values!

A quick review of boolean operations may be in order, because of their importance in programming. There are several important operations that can be performed on Boolean values: AND, OR, NOT, and XOR. With the exception of NOT operations, all Boolean operations take two TRUE or FALSE values and determine an answer, based on these values and on the operation (AND, OR, XOR) being performed.

The AND operation returns a TRUE value if *both* values are TRUE. As shown in this illustration, the two input values can be thought of as two switches in series; if the first one AND the second one are on, then the output will be on.

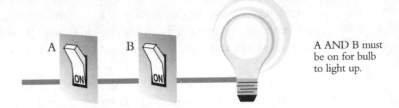

A AND B must be on for bulb to light up.

The OR operation returns a result of TRUE if either of the two input values are TRUE. As shown in the following illustration, the two values in an OR operation can be thought of as two switches in parallel; if the first input OR the second input are on, then the output will be on.

A OR B must be on for bulb to light up.

The XOR (or *exclusive*-or) operation assigns a TRUE value only if the two input values are not the same. The NOT operation simply reverses a TRUE or FALSE value (that is, NOT TRUE is FALSE, and NOT FALSE is TRUE).

Figures 2–4 summarizes the output of these operations, given the various possible input values.

Building Your Own Data Types

Most computer programs store data in *variables*. Variables are simply places in the computer's memory where data can be stored. Each variable has an assigned data type so that the correct amount of computer storage space can be reserved.

Figure 2-4

Output of the AND, OR, XOR, and NOT operations

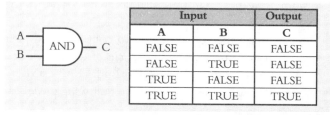

	Input		Output	
	A	**B**	**C**	
	FALSE	FALSE	FALSE	Results of AND operations
	FALSE	TRUE	FALSE	
	TRUE	FALSE	FALSE	
	TRUE	TRUE	TRUE	

	Input		Output	
	A	**B**	**C**	
	FALSE	FALSE	FALSE	Results of OR operations
	FALSE	TRUE	TRUE	
	TRUE	FALSE	TRUE	
	TRUE	TRUE	TRUE	

	Input		Output	
	A	**B**	**C**	
	FALSE	FALSE	FALSE	Results of XOR operations
	FALSE	TRUE	TRUE	
	TRUE	FALSE	TRUE	
	TRUE	TRUE	FALSE	

Input	Output	
A	**C**	
FALSE	TRUE	Results of NOT operations
TRUE	FALSE	

Generally, computer languages have built-in data types that correspond with most of the types you've read about in this chapter. At times, however, you may wish to create new types of your own. This is a common practice with Boolean values. Some languages do not have an actual data type for Booleans; they just use the numbers 1 and 0 for TRUE and FALSE. To make your programs more easily deciphered by the human eye, you may want to create your own data type, called "Boolean." The process of creating new data types is described in Chapter 4.

Another reason for creating your own data types is to collect data about something and store it all in one place. If you write a payroll program, for example, you may wish to store all the information about an employee in one location. For these purposes, structured data types are made available by many languages.

Structured variables allow you to collect related pieces of information and store them together as one big article of data. For instance, suppose that you create a program to track your Christmas card list. For each person or family on your list, you want to record the following pieces of information:

◆ Name

◆ Street Address

◆ City

◆ State

◆ ZIP code

◆ The last year you received a card from them

To move this information around your program with standard data types would require six steps each time (one step for each piece of information). However, if you create a structured data type with spaces for six pieces of data, you'll be able to move the entire block of information at one time. This advantage may not be completely clear yet, but it will be discussed in more detail in Chapter 4.

How Long Does Data Last?

Another question you may ask is, "How long is data available in a program?" The answer is that you make data last as long as you need to. Programming languages offer two basic data storage items for specifying the length of time that an element of data will have a specific value.

Variables are used to represent storage locations in the computer. Each variable has an associated data type, and values of that type may be placed into the designated storage location at any time. Variables can have values assigned to them, like the ones in this example:

```
Name = "John Smith"
Total = 100.54
```

Variables such as **Name** and **Total** can be assigned new values during the execution of the program. However, there may be values that must remain the same during the entire program, or forever. To let you store these permanent values, programming languages allow you to designate *constant* variables.

Constants are used to maintain values that will remain unchanging, throughout every use of your program. For instance, you would not want to write a mathematical modeling program that allowed the value of pi (3.1415926...) to change each time the program ran!

Constants cannot be controlled by the programmer; these values never change during a program. In Pascal, these values are assigned in the CONST section of the program, while variables are defined in the VAR section. In the example below, notice how much easier it is to read **pi** than **3.1415926**.

remember: *In your programs, variables can be varied, but constants remain constant!*

```
CONST
   pi = 3.1415926;

VAR
   InNum : Real;
   Total : Real;

BEGIN
   Write("What is your number? ");
   Readln(InNum);
   Total := InNum * pi;
   Writeln("The total is ", Total);
END.
```

Moving Data In and Out of a Program

To get information into your program and out of it again, computer languages provide input and output functions. These will be defined here briefly. The different kinds of statements that you can use in your programs to control input and output will be discussed more fully in Chapters 4 and 7.

Computer Lingo

A statement is a single command written in your program. All programs, are made up of a series of statements. Statements are used for assigning values to variables and controlling input and output, as well as for processing information and managing the sequence of events in your programs (as you will learn in Chapters 4 and 5).

Input

Input is the process of getting data into your program. The two most common means of input are the computer keyboard and the disk drives. However, you might also receive input via your system's serial ports; these ports can connect your system to a bar code scanner or other data source; they can also be used to connect your computer to other computers, directly or through a modem. A connection to a computer network allows input from other people on the network (if you permit it!).

Output

Output is the information that results when your program is run. Output is usually sent to the computer screen or a printer for viewing, or to a disk drive for storage. But again, a network or serial port connection widens these possibilities to include other computers, bar code printers, or overhead display systems. You might also output information to a service company, who would then use it to create color slides for a presentation. (This type of data transfer could be done with a disk, through a network connection, or via modem on your serial port.)

Communicating with the Computer

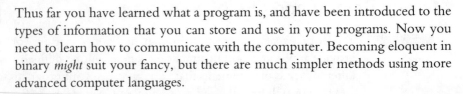

Thus far you have learned what a program is, and have been introduced to the types of information that you can store and use in your programs. Now you need to learn how to communicate with the computer. Becoming eloquent in binary *might* suit your fancy, but there are much simpler methods using more advanced computer languages.

Chapter 3

Learning a New Language

Prince Wang's programmer was coding software. His fingers
danced upon the keyboard. The program compiled without an error
message, and the program ran like a gentle wind.

"Excellent!" the Prince exclaimed, "Your technique is faultless!"

"Technique?" said the programmer turning from his terminal, "What I
follow is Tao—beyond all techniques! When I first began to program I
would see before me the whole problem in one mass. After three
years I no longer saw this mass. Instead, I used subroutines. But now,
I see nothing. My whole being exists in a formless void. My senses
are idle.

"My spirit, free to work without plan, follows its own instinct. In short,
my program writes itself. True, sometimes there are difficult
problems. I see them coming, I slow down, I watch silently. Then I
change a single line of code and the difficulties vanish like puffs of
idle smoke. I then compile the program. I sit still and let the joy of the
work fill my being. I close my eyes for a moment and then log off."

Prince Wang said, "Would that all my programmers were as wise!"

— The Tao of Programming

I N order to start programming, you need to select a programming language. In
some cases, this decision will be made for you: Your boss or client may select
the language, or you may only have one language available. But as you gain
more programming experience, you will want to look at the different languages
available, and make the choice for each project based on the relative merits of
each language.

In this chapter, you'll learn how programming languages work and what some of them look like. You'll also find out how to determine the best language to use for a specific project. A more in-depth look at some of the languages mentioned in this chapter is presented in Appendix C.

An Introduction to Programming Languages

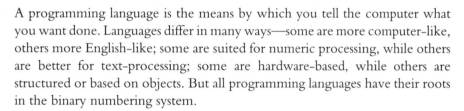

A programming language is the means by which you tell the computer what you want done. Languages differ in many ways—some are more computer-like, others more English-like; some are suited for numeric processing, while others are better for text-processing; some are hardware-based, while others are structured or based on objects. But all programming languages have their roots in the binary numbering system.

Binary and Hex Programming

The earliest computers were programmed through a process that involved manually flipping switches on front of the computer. Each of the switches was a specific bit, and each one was turned on or off by the operator. Can you imagine inputting a program that way today, when some applications come with 50 megabytes of programs and utilities? That would be the equivalent of flipping 400,000,000 switches!

An early program may have been as simple as this:

```
110101110101000101001001010
```

which is relatively short, but not very easy to read.

Of course, the earlier computers would not have had enough memory or storage to handle current programs. Some of the first computers had 256 *bytes* of memory, as compared with common PCs of today with 4 or 8 *megabytes* of memory! Disk space wasn't even available at first; it hadn't been invented yet.

note: *One of the consequences of low storage availability was the use of special cards called* punched cards. *For many years, there was no room to store the program source code in computer memory or disk space, so the only way to program was to store this data on punched cards. Each of these oversized index cards had one line of source code or data encoded in a series of holes punched into the card; the cards were punched on a special* keypunch *machine, and read into the computer* *using a card reader. The compilers read one card at a time, generating an object file from this input. Naturally, because they contained source code, the cards had to be kept in a strict order. Programmers could often be seen carrying boxes of these cards around. Dropping a box of punched cards was equivalent to a hard disk crash in today's programming environment; you could recreate the source code from a program listing, but it meant retyping all of the code.*

As computers grew, and programming tasks became more complex, new methods were devised for entering programs. At this time, only numeric digits were allowed. Octal numbers were used first; a digit in an octal number represents three bits. Hexadecimal numbers followed, allowing a programmer to enter eight bits as only two characters in a program.

It was still very difficult to read and write programs, because they appeared only as strings of digits and hex characters, like this:

```
47 1F 8B C3 48 50 8B C6 F7 D0 2B D0 50
```

While at first glance, this is not much simpler to read than binary code, hex programming did provide some advantages. First, the programs became much shorter, since each hex digit represents four bits of binary code. Second, commands were becoming easier to recognize and remember; a programmer could pick out that "47" was a move command, and "50" was an addition. This was the first step toward the higher-level programming languages in use today. Programmers who were not into their work full-time, however, often found themselves forgetting these codes, so hex programming did not solve all their problems.

Assembly Language Programming

The next step in programming evolution was the development of special programs which read a more English-like programming language, and then generated corresponding binary code for the computer to work with. These programs were called *assemblers*, because they were designed to *assemble* a program for the computer from the commands entered by the user. The language used to input these commands was called *assembly language*.

Assembly language programs are much simpler to read than binary or hex programs. For instance, the hex example shown above can be written in assembly code as follows:

```
INC DI
POP DS
MOV AX,BX
```

```
DEC AX
PUSH AX
MOV AX,SI
NOT AX
SUB DX,AX
PUSH AX
```

This is still not much like your everyday language, but at least **SUB** is more like the word subtract than is **2B**. The names you see in this example (**AX**, **BX**, **DS**, **DI**, etc.) are built-in names for *registers,* which are special memory locations in the computer that are often used in programs. These names are also easier to use and remember than are their numeric representations.

Many people today still work in assembly language. Since it is closer to the language the computer understands, it is very powerful. When programmers first started using high-level languages (such as FORTRAN, Pascal, and C), code written in assembly language still had performance increases of 10 to 100 times over the "high-level" equivalent.

note:

Although assembly language is possibly still the most powerful tool for programming, it is not used for most programming projects. Why? A good compiler will produce machine code that is on par with that of an expert assembly language programmer. Keep in mind that most assembly programmers are not experienced experts; in other words, while the very best assembly programmers can write code that runs faster, and that uses less memory, than the code generated by compilers, not many programmers fall into the "very best" category. These days, you generally get better code from a high-level language compiler!

But assembly language still had its limitations. With the early assemblers, you needed to remember the exact locations in the computer's memory where you stored information; assigning variable names to storage locations (detailed in Chapter 4) was not yet a common practice. Also, the input and output processes were very rigorous—not at all simple or straightforward (except to diehard assembly language programmers, of course). So further refinement was needed.

High-Level Languages

Once assemblers hit, programmers found that they could work much more quickly and accurately. The next step was to use these assemblers to build even more advanced programs. These programs would take an even more English-like programming language and convert it into binary code for the computer.

Many of these "high-level" languages were developed, and are still being developed and improved.

Some of the earliest languages were FORTRAN (named for FORmula TRANslation), used for numeric processing; COBOL (COmmon Business Oriented Language), used for batch transaction processing and reporting; and BASIC (Beginner's All-purpose Symbolic Instruction Code), used as a teaching language. LISP (LISt Processing) was also used in many educational settings.

More recent programming languages include Smalltalk, C and C++, Pascal, Modula-2, and Visual Basic. Many of the earlier languages were developed specifically for one purpose. Now, languages have a more rounded appeal, so that programmers are not forced to move from language to language to language in order to complete projects with varied needs. And many of the older languages have been changed to meet the demands of a new generation of programmers.

Here are some examples of how these programs might look:

FORTRAN

```
      PROGRAM TestF
C     This is a comment

C     Define Variable
      CHARACTER*30 NAME

      READ(*,*) NAME
      WRITE(100,*) 'Hello there, ', NAME

      END
```

BASIC

```
REM This is a comment (or REMark)
INPUT Name$
PRINT "Hello there, ", Name$
```

C

```
#include <stdio.h>
```

```
/* This is a comment */

/* Define variable */
char name[30];

main()
{
   scanf("%s", name);
   printf("Hello there, %s\n", name);
}
```

C++

```
#include <iostream.h>

/* This is one type of comment */

// Define Variable (another comment type)
char name[30];

main()
{
   cin >> name;   // this is another comment
   cout << "Hello there, " << name << eoln;
}
```

Pascal

```
Program TestP;

{ This is a comment }

(* Define variable (another comment type) *)
VAR
   name : String;

BEGIN
   readln(name);
   write("Hello there, ");
   writeln(name);
END
```

Modula-2

```
MODULE TestM;

(* This is a comment *)

(* Define variable *)
Name : ARRAY[1..30] OF CHARACTER;

BEGIN
   Read(Name);
   WriteStr("Hello there, ");
   WriteStr(Name);
   WriteLn();
END TestM.
```

Although each of these examples uses a different structure and wording, they all accomplish basically the same functions: asking the user of the program for their name, and then writing "Hello there," followed by the name just read.

These languages are commonly known as *third-generation languages,* or 3GLs. These are the types of languages you will learn about throughout the rest of this book. The knowledge you gain, however, will be applicable to fourth-generation languages as well.

note: *Although the newest languages are called* third-generation, *the earlier languages never really used the names* first-generation *and* second-generation. *(Think of it this way: The first World War didn't need a number until the second one happened.) Even so, the first generation of computer programming involved binary and hex code, while assembly language programming, being slightly more like the English language, brought us into the second generation. This continued evolution has lead to the third generation, where actual English words are used.*

4GL and Database Languages

Fourth-generation languages, or 4GLs, are designed to simplify programming for the beginning or part-time programmer. Many of the 4GLs offer features that prevent programmers from having to perform many of the same tasks over and over.

Many of the 4GLs are based on a database concept. Thus, if you build a lot of programs that need a database, a 4GL can probably perform many of your day-to-day programming chores, freeing you to do the customization required for each project.

A 4GL allows you to specify the files that you will be using, the *fields* (pieces of data) that you'll need to access in each file, and how the files are related (for example, each person in the **EMPLOYEE** file may have an associated record in the **BOSS** file, one in the **PAYROLL** file, and one or more records in the **PROJECTS** file).

Some of the more common database languages include xBase (used with the dBASE, FoxPro, FoxBase, and Clipper programs), PAL (used with Paradox), and Clarion. There are also many 4GLs not tied directly to database programs. If this level of programming language is something you would like to learn more about, you may wish to browse through some of the database magazines listed in Appendix D.

Compilers vs. Interpreters

Computers can only execute binary code. Therefore, the ultimate goal of any programming language must be the generation of binary code.

Compilers directly generate binary programs, ready to run. To create a compiled program, you must write the program, save it, run it through the compiler, and then see if it works. If there are problems (and there usually are, at least for a while), you must edit the program and then compile it over again. This process can be time-consuming; however, once you compile your program, anyone who wants to use it can do so without having to use any additional software.

Compiled languages go through several steps each time you make a change to your program. First, the code is compiled into a binary format. Then it is linked to various *libraries* (these are common pieces of code that are used in virtually all programs). Finally, the program is compiled into a complete binary program that is ready for the computer to run. This sequence of operations can be simplified with an interpreter, but at a cost.

Interpreters run your code line by line, as it is being written. When you use an interpreter, you know immediately when there are problems, instead of having to wait until the program is complete. However, interpreted programs run much more slowly than do compiled programs. Interpreted languages do generate binary code, but each line of each program is interpreted *each time* the program runs. There is no compiling step for transforming your whole program, *once and for all*, into binary. Therefore, another drawback to programming with an interpreter is that before anyone can use your program, they must also have the interpreter.

The interpretive process does not require a linking step, because the common libraries are always kept available when the program runs. This makes the programming process simpler, but does not allow for much *extensibility* (the ability to add new commands to the language).

The common languages available with compilers include C and C++, Pascal, Modula-2, FORTRAN, COBOL, Smalltalk, Lisp, and more recently, BASIC. Some of these are also included in the list of available interpretive languages: BASIC, C, Pascal, and others.

As a result of this diversity, two changes have taken place to improve the programming industry. First, many of the languages that used to be available only as interpreters (BASIC, for instance) started to show up as compilers. (One example of this is the BASIC language packaged with MS-DOS; in versions 1.0 through 5.0 of MS-DOS, the GWBASIC interpreter was supplied, while version 6.0 comes with the QBASIC compiler.) Second, compiler vendors, anxious to offer the flexibility of interpreters, have begun marketing developing packages that tie the edit-compile-run cycle into one integrated environment. (An example is shown in Figure 3-1).

As you can see in this figure, you get much more from a programming environment than just being able to write and edit source code. Simply click one of the graphic icons with your mouse to start debugging your program,

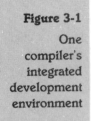

Figure 3-1

One compiler's integrated development environment

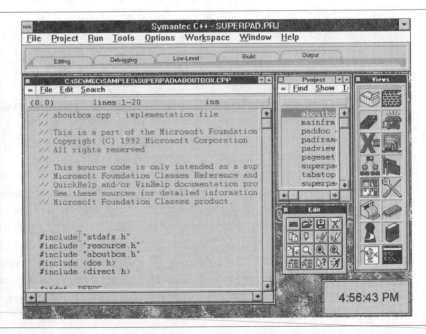

build an executable program, or look at the output that is generated by your program. You can look at each of the different files that make up your programming project; you can even run your program by making a simple menu selection.

Specialty Languages

Beyond compilers and interpreters for programmers, several other types of language products have appeared. These include batch programs (or control or command files), and specialized dialects of standard programming languages.

BATCH, COMMAND, AND SCRIPT FILES

Almost every computer environment now available provides some sort of interpretive language designed to help you set up and control your system.

PC-DOS and MS-DOS systems use *batch files* to relay commands to the operating system. Batch files always have the .BAT file extension. A batch file might look like this:

```
REM Batch File to backup document files
ECHO OFF
ECHO Please put the backup disk in A: and
REM Pause will display "Press any key to continue"
PAUSE
FOR %%I IN (DOC DRW DAT) DO COPY *.%%I A:
ECHO Finished. Please put backup disk away.
```

These types of commands are also available under OS/2, but they are stored in *command files* (.CMD), so that OS/2-specific commands can be used.

Unix-based operating systems use *scripts*, or *shell scripts*. These are similar in concept to batch and command files, but look somewhat different. A script file might look like this:

```
stty erase '^h' -tabs
MAIL=/usr/spool/mail/john
PATH=:$HOME/bin:/bin:/usr/bin
TERM=vt100
c=$HOME/source
export MAIL PATH TERM c
date
who | wc -1
```

LANGUAGE DIALECTS

Many of the newer, high-power software applications include their own languages, used for customizing the programs and for creating procedures that can be performed over and over without undue burden on program users. Often these languages are called *macro* languages, and the programs written with them are called *macros*.

For example, if you need to move a column of information in a file, you can write a macro that moves the column in one row of the file, and then run the macro on the entire file, changing each line without your further intervention. In a spreadsheet program, you might write a macro to calculate the internal rate of return on an investment, based on numbers entered into the spreadsheet by the user. Since you will not want to calculate the IRR until all the numbers are entered, you might automatically start the macro after the user has finished entering data; the user won't even realize that the calculations are taking place, but they will see the final answer.

Most macro languages are dialects, or subsets, of standard programming languages, notably BASIC and C. Many text editors designed specifically for programmers provide macro features, usually using a dialect derived from the C language. This is useful for performing repetitive tasks.

Microsoft is using Visual Basic as the language basis for a programming environment consistent across all their Windows-based applications, including Excel and Word for Windows. LotusScript is used in the Lotus Improv spreadsheet program. Lotus Ami Pro is also programmable.

Of course, almost all spreadsheet programs, including Lotus 1-2-3, Microsoft Excel, and Borland Quattro Pro, provide macro languages that allow users to streamline their spreadsheet operations.

Three Popular Programming Languages

Three programming languages that are quite popular in the United States, and in many parts of the world, are BASIC, Pascal, and C/C++. Throughout the rest of this book, these languages will be used to show examples of the concepts you are learning. If you learn to read these languages, you will be ready to tackle nearly any programming task.

First, a short introduction to all three languages is in order.

BASIC

BASIC (Beginner's All-purpose Symbolic Instruction Code) has been available since the early 1960s. BASIC has been included with MS-DOS, in one form or another, since the introduction of the IBM PC. In fact, many of the first programs written for the IBM PC were written in BASIC. However, in the first versions of MS-DOS, BASIC was interpreted rather than compiled, so programs written in BASIC had a tendency to execute very slowly.

Early BASIC programs had many other limitations as well. Some of these problems are shown in this example:

```
10 A=1
20 A=A*2
30 B=A+1
40 C=5
50 D=A+B+C
60 IF B<C GOTO 20
70 PRINT "A=", A, " B=", B, " C=", C
80 PRINT "D=", D
```

In this program, you can see that the names **A**, **B**, and **C** are used; many of the first BASIC implementations had a one or two character limit on variable names due to memory restrictions. However, there is little in the program that tells you what **A**, **B**, and **C** are used for. To compound this problem, early programming rarely had good comments. (This was true in other languages as well as BASIC.) Finally, early BASIC required every line in a program to be numbered. If you needed to add another line to the program, you had to fit the number between those already used, or renumber all the lines that followed!

Over time, however, BASIC has evolved to where it is now much faster and easier to work with. The newer BASIC products contain compilers, so programs created with them are able to run much more quickly. Variable names can be any length, and line numbers are no longer required. With Visual Basic, in particular, a lot of exciting programming is being done in both Windows and DOS, by people who might never have become programmers without such a tool.

In Visual Basic, much of the process of developing an application involves manipulation of the graphical elements of the application (menus and screens, and the items on the screens). Although some code must still be entered manually, Visual Basic offers an environment that can be less cryptic and more inviting than purely text-based programming languages. In addition, Visual Basic implements some aspects of object-oriented programming (OOP), one of the latest software development technologies. Object-oriented programming, is described in detail in Chapter 8; its value is that it allows many people to better understand programming in terms of everyday objects they may be familiar with.

Although BASIC was originally designed as a beginning, or training language, it has finally grown into a professional development tool—although some programmers might not like to admit it!

note: *Many programmers who started working with the IBM PC in the early 1980s had no practical option but to program in BASIC; it was the first language supplied with the PC, and there was no additional cost required for using it. But as BASIC programs became more and more complex, they became a nightmare to maintain. GOTO statements made it extremely difficult to follow a program's flow. Ultimately, many programmers switched to Turbo Pascal; others put their money into more expensive compilers. Once they left BASIC, many programmers came to look upon it as a toy, for learning only (even though they had created some wonderful programs under BASIC). Now BASIC has matured into a more structured language, without line numbers, and with elegant alternatives to the aggravating GOTO statement. Is it still a toy language? Some perceptions never change, even when they're based on old information.*

Computer Lingo

Structured programming is the process of designing and writing programs in a modularized, methodical format. In structured programming, the use of **GOTO** statements is reduced or even eliminated through the use of looping and control statements. Large programs are broken down into smaller sections, each of which performs a single function.

Pascal

Nikolaus Wirth designed Pascal as a teaching language, showing how a structured design could be implemented in a computer language. BASIC, at the time, was not at all a structured language.

You may remember this spaghetti code example from the BASIC discussion above:

```
10  A=1
20  A=A*2
30  B=A+1
40  C=5
50  D=A+B+C
60  IF B<C GOTO 20
70  PRINT "A=", A, " B=", B, " C=", C
80  PRINT "D=", D
```

Changing this program excerpt into a Pascal program shows the components of Pascal that add structure to computer code:

```
Pascal Program 1;

VAR
    A, B, C, D : Integer;

BEGIN
    A := 1;
    REPEAT
        A := A * 2;
        B := A + 1;
        C := 5;
        D := A + B + C;
    UNTIL B >= C;
    Write("A= ", A, " B= ", B, " C= ", C );
    Writeln(" D= ", D );
END.
```

While this example still suffers from short variable names and a lack of comments, you can quickly see how structuring the code makes it much more understandable. Take a moment to examine the basic structure of this: in Pascal, variables are declared in one area, and commands are placed in another.

Pascal became popular in many schools in Europe (where Wirth lives). Eventually, Wirth saw that what he had designed as a teaching language was being used for professional development. Unfortunately, at that time it did not support large programs very well; all of the code had to be recompiled each time a change was made. He redesigned Pascal and produced Modula-2, developed to overcome the shortcomings in Pascal. Modula-2 introduced the concept of *modules,* which are sections of code that can be compiled separately, and finally combined to form complete programs.

A few years later, Wirth developed Oberon, which changed Modula-2 into a smaller, object-oriented language. These languages have done well in Europe and other parts of the world, but not nearly as well in the United States. This probably has to do with the fact that Pascal, Modula-2, and Oberon were developed in Europe, while C and C++ were born in the U.S.

In the early 1980s, Borland International introduced Turbo Pascal. This new product really took off, with good reason: For less than $50, you could now get a complete Pascal development system, including an editor and a compiler. Not only did these new tools make code development less painful, the compiler was very fast!

This was a major change in the PC programming world. Previously, most of the compilers available cost between $400 and $1500. Most of these did not include an editor, not to mention an integrated environment. Plus, the Turbo Pascal compiler was by far the fastest available, and the programs that it generated were also some of the fastest available. What did you pay for this outstanding package? $49!

Building on this excellent start, Turbo Pascal has since emerged as the de facto standard for Pascal programmers worldwide. This compiler environment is available for DOS, Macintosh, and Windows environments. Other Pascal compilers are available, and many of them are very good. But Turbo Pascal started the ball rolling, and has kept ahead of the pack ever since.

C/C++

The C programming language was originally developed by AT&T Bell Labs for use in their telephone switching systems. The C language was also used to write the Unix operating system. Consequently, Unix shell commands often look similar to C code.

The following C program performs the same functions as the preceding Pascal example:

```
int A, B, C, D;

main()
{
   A = 1;
   for (A=1; B<C; )
   {
```

```
      A = A * 2;
      B = A + 1;
      C = 5;
      D = A + B + C;
   }
  printf("A= %d B= %d C= %d", A, B, C );
  printf(" D= %d \n", D );
}
```

C may seem to be more cryptic than Pascal, but this comes from a desire to avoid cluttering the language with undue verbosity. Once you understand C syntax (the language itself), you will quickly see the power that is available with this language.

For many years, C was often considered a replacement for assembly code. C compilers worked so well that the code they generated was nearly as good as code that a professional assembly language programmer might write by hand; the code was automatically optimized for speed, and it used the least memory possible. Now, other languages are catching up in capability, but C and C++ are well established as the languages of choice for systems-level programming.

C has numerous strengths in dealing with data, as you will begin to see in the next chapter. Whatever you need to accomplish with a programming language, C can do it for you. The C language offers great flexibility because it puts the programmer in complete control. However, with that type of power comes a price: you can do things in C that you won't be aware of at first. As you continue through this book, you will learn about some errors that are commonly made by C programmers.

C++ was designed as an upgrade to C, adding object-oriented programming capabilities. C++ compilers will generally compile any C code that you have written; in this way, they provide a simple upgrade path. Once you learn C, C++ can be taught mostly through the concepts of objects, as discussed in Chapter 8.

Choosing a Language

Choosing a programming language used to be a relatively simple matter. Business reporting and batch-transaction-based programs used COBOL. Programs requiring a lot of mathematical calculations depended on FORTRAN. Programs with a great deal of string manipulation used Pascal. Utilities and system-control programs used C.

But then the question of portability came out. Was FORTRAN on a PC the same as FORTRAN on a Vax, or on a Cray? Unfortunately, the answer was no. BASIC was probably the worst culprit, with nearly every vendor changing all but the most fundamental commands.

FORTRAN become standardized in the 1960s and 1970s, and the standards have continued to be revised. C has finally been standardized through ANSI (the American National Standards Institute), and C++ will soon follow. BASIC may never be standardized in a popular form; everyone wants to add their own bells and whistles.

Computer Lingo

Bells and whistles are additional features added to a program to make it just a little better than the rest.

Pascal has a standard, but most people follow the de facto Turbo Pascal standard. For instance, about the time that Wirth designed Modula-2, Borland added many of the same revisions to their Pascal compilers, even though the Pascal standard never added the same new features.

So how do you choose a language? First, decide where your program needs to run. If you want to support a great number of computers, you may look to C, as C is now available on almost every computer made.

Second, decide what type of program you need to write. FORTRAN and COBOL have been around a long time, and there is probably more code written in these two languages than in any other. But they have their strength and their weaknesses. If your program will revolve around database manipulation, a 4GL or database language may be a good choice.

Third, determine what support you will need, and if it is available. If you use C or Turbo Pascal, for instance, you can buy libraries (code that has already been written, and that can be used in your programs) that generate graphics, perform numerical calculations, and carry out many other functions. Using libraries will save you a lot of time in the long run. However, if you select a language or compiler that does not have good support in the industry, you'll end up doing everything yourself. For all but the smallest applications, this is not usually a great way to program!

Finally, examine the languages themselves and see which one you feel most comfortable with. This book will introduce you to some of the more common programming languages. Once you select one or two that look good, you may wish to read a book that deals specifically with the language or languages you are interested in before you make your final decision.

Chapter 4

Using Information in Your

Programs

A novice asked the master: "Here is a programmer who never designs, documents, or tests his programs. Yet all who know him consider him one of the best programmers in the world. Why is this?"

The master replied: "That programmer has mastered the Tao. He has gone beyond the need for design; he does not become angry when the system crashes, but accepts the universe without concern. He has gone beyond the need for testing; each of him programs are perfect within themselves, serene and elegant, their purpose self-evident.

"Truly, he has entered the mystery of Tao."

—The Tao of Programming

S O far, you have learned about the kinds of data that can be utilized in your programs. You have also been introduced to the types of languages that are available. In this chapter, you will begin learning how programs are put together, examining real examples in three languages: BASIC, Pascal, and C.

We will begin with a discussion of programming style. You'll be introduced to different methods for managing data, as used by computer programs written in BASIC, Pascal, and C. You will also learn how information can be gathered from the outside world and used in your computer programs, and how the results of your programs can be made known outside of the computer.

note: *This chapter is a very high-level overview of the capabilities of Pascal, BASIC, and C. It is by no means a complete introduction to any of the languages. More complete examples of programs written in these languages are presented in Chapter 7.*

Your Programming Style

Programming style is the manner in which you lay out code in a source file. Programming style is extremely important, but is not stressed often enough.

Computer Lingo

The commands and statements that you enter in your chosen language—the program that you write—is called *source code*. Your source code filenames will always end with the file extensions specific to the language you use (.C for C programs, .PAS for Pascal, .BAS for BASIC, .FOR for FORTRAN, .COB for COBOL, .CPP for C++, etc.).

When your source code is compiled, *object code* is produced. It is usually found in files that end with the .OBJ extension. When you link the object files together, you create *executable code*, the actual program that can be run. Executable code filenames end in .EXE or .COM.

Some languages have rigid specifications for the way that code must be formatted. For instance, many FORTRAN compilers require that you start program statements in column 7 or greater. A comment marker can only be placed in column 6, and line numbers appear in columns 1 through 5. The RPG language uses fixed columns on each line of code to mean different things.

Other languages, like Pascal and C, are very flexible when it comes to the format of your code—they require almost *nothing*! Therefore, you need to choose your own guidelines, and train yourself to follow them.

You will begin to develop a personalized style of programming as you become more experienced. This is true for any programming language; if you don't establish guidelines for yourself, you may end up writing code that even you will not be able to read. Programming style is mostly just a matter of being consistent, especially in the areas of indentation, comments, and variable names.

The following sections offer examples of different programming styles. Use a style that suits you, or modify one of these styles to create your own. But be consistent! Consistency in your programming style will prove invaluable when you return later to re-read your code. It will also enable other programmers to read your code with minimal confusion.

tip:

Don't feel that you need to make decisions about your style immediately. Try the different techniques shown here, and then add changes as you see fit. Your programming style will continually evolve as you program, but do be careful to ensure that it remains consistent at any one time, within any one program or project.

Indentation

The Pascal and C languages do not require any specific style of formatting or indentation; the format that you use is entirely up to you. Below are some examples of how other programmers have decided to indent their work.

Indentation shows how blocks of code are combined. There are numerous ways to use blocks, and most blocks are surrounded by *delimiters* that show where each block begins and ends: C uses the brace symbols { and }, while Pascal uses the **BEGIN** and **END** commands. As you look through the examples that follow, be sure to examine how the blocks of code are indented.

The number of spaces that you choose to indent is also a matter of style, although most programmers find that indenting two to four spaces per level of indentation is sufficient.

Decide on a pattern of indentation that looks right to you, and then use it consistently. One option is to place all statements in a block of code which is indented from the *controlling* part of the block (that is, the statement that determines whether the block will be executed. The controlling statement is usually found at the top of the block). The delimiters are not indented. This style is demonstrated here, first in C and then in Pascal:

C

```
/*
    C program showing the first indentation style
    By: L. John Ribar, Programming Primer
*/
#include <stdio.h>

main()
{
    int a, b;

    a = 1;
    b = a + 1;
    printf("a is equal to 1 \n");
```

```
if (b==1)
{
    printf("b is also equal to 1 \n");
    a = b * 3;
}
else
{
    printf("b is not equal to 1 \n");
    b = a * 3;
}

printf("a is now equal to %d \n", a);
printf("b is now equal to %d \n", b);
}
```

Pascal

```
(*
    Pascal program showing the first indentation style
    By: L. John Ribar, Programming Primer
*)
Program Indent1;

Uses CRT;    (* allow input and output *)

VAR
    a, b : Integer;

BEGIN

    a := 1;
    b := a + 1;
    Writeln("a is equal to 1");
    IF b=1 THEN
    BEGIN
        Writeln("b is also equal to 1");
        a := b * 3;
    END
    ELSE
    BEGIN
        Writeln("b is not equal to 1");
        b := a * 3;
    END
```

```
Write("a is now equal to ");
Writeln(a);
Write("b is now equal to ");
Writeln(b);

END (* of program *)
```

A second indentation option involves indenting the delimiters (**BEGIN** and **END**, or braces) along with the indented code. Here is an example of a C program using this format:

```
/*
   C program showing the second indentation style
   By: L. John Ribar, Programming Primer
*/

#include <stdio.h>

main ()
   {
   int a, b;

   a = 1;
   b = a + 1;
   printf("a is equal to 1 \n");
   if (b==1)
      {
      printf("b is also equal to 1 \n");
      a = b * 3;
      }
   else
      {
      printf("b is not equal to 1 \n");
      b = a * 3;
      }
   }
```

A third indentation option involves moving the first block delimiter (the **BEGIN** or opening brace) onto the line of code preceding the block of code. An example of this style in Pascal is shown here:

```
(*
    Pascal program showing the third indentation style
    By: L. John Ribar, Programming Primer
*)
Program Indent3;

Uses CRT;    (* allow input and output *)

VAR
    a, b : Integer;

BEGIN

    a := 1;
    b := a + 1;
    Writeln("a is equal to 1");
    IF b=1 THEN BEGIN
        Writeln("b is also equal to 1");
        a := b * 3;
    END
    ELSE BEGIN
        Writeln("b is not equal to 1");
        b := a * 3;
    END

    Write("a is now equal to ");
    Writeln(a);
    Write("b is now equal to ");
    Writeln(b);

END (* of program *)
```

The point here is that any of these styles is perfectly acceptable, as long as it is used consistently. Throughout the rest of this book, we will use the first two styles illustrated in this chapter.

Comments

While comments are very important in all programming (and especially with languages as flexible and free-form as C), they are often ignored or played down by programmers. This is because comments are not part of the code necessary for making the program work, and therefore do not appear to be as important.

note: *Comments are not required in programs. You should, however, try to get into the habit of commenting your code. Although this may not seem important when you are writing a program—and may, in fact, seem like an extra chore—your comments will be extremely valuable when you come back later and try to decipher what you have written.*

Comments do not need to be lengthy, but they do need to explain what is happening in the program. This should be plain enough so that you, the programmer, or other users will be able to understand the code in the future. It is not necessary, or even desirable, to comment each line of code. However, you should put comments in the following places:

◆ **At the beginning of the file** These comments describe what is in the file, possibly who wrote it and when, and any other files that it may be linked to or dependent upon. In addition, it is often helpful to add the compiler and version used, and the steps required for building the program (the compiler and linker commands, etc.).

◆ **At the beginning of each function** A *function* is a named piece of code that can be called (or started) from other places in your program, and that usually performs a single task. Function comments describe how the function is called, what it does, and what parameters are used with it. *Parameters* are the values or variables sent into and returned from functions. (Functions will be discussed further in Chapter 6.)

◆ **In any area where the algorithms are not straightforward** These comments will later help you remember why things were done in a particular way.

Computer Lingo

The series of steps necessary to perform a given task is called an *algorithm*. For instance, two common programming methods used to search for a given item in a list involve two different algorithms.

If the items in the list are not in order (numeric or alphabetical), you need to use a sequential search. This type of search does not require a complex algorithm; the computer simply starts at the top of the list and looks at each item until it finds the one you have specified.

If the items are in order, you can use a binary search. The algorithm for this procedure involves repeatedly splitting the list in half, and then eliminating each half until the desired answer is located in the half being searched. The algorithm for a binary search is more complex than that for a sequential search; if you use a binary search in one of your programs, it should be commented (so that when you examine the code later, you'll remember how it is supposed to work).

Each language has its own rules for adding comments. In C, comments start with two characters: a backslash and an asterisk (/*), with no spaces between them. C comments end with the same two characters *in reversed order* (*/). In Pascal, comments are surrounded in a similar way, either with the (* and *) combination or simply with braces, { and }.

In BASIC, a comment line begins with **REM** (short for Remark). Optionally, a BASIC comment can start anywhere in a line, if it begins with the apostrophe character ('). When this method is used, the comment continues to the end of the line.

In some languages (like C and Pascal), comments can be written on a single line or can cross multiple lines. Comments may contain any characters except additional comments. (Comments within comments, called *nested comments,* are not allowed.) The following example, written in Pascal, shows comments on single lines and comments crossing several lines.

```
(*
   Function to determine a big number

   This function returns a number that is all the
   numbers equal to or less than i, multiplied
   together. For instance, if i=3, then this
   function will return 1*2*3, or 6.
```

```
     Input:     The base number, i
     Output:    The big number
*)

Function BigNumber( i : Integer ) : Integer;
VAR
   big : Integer;
BEGIN
   big := 1;  (* start out with 1 *)

   (* Multiply for each number. Skip 1 since
      multiplying by 1 doesn't change the
      result. *)
   FOR count := 2 TO i DO
     big := big * count;
   END;
   RETURN big;  (* send the number back *)

END; (* function *)
```

While you may not yet understand *how* this example works, notice how the comments help you to better understand *what* is happening. Also notice that the format of a comment can change from line to line; some comments are one a single line, while others span several lines. How you format your comments will be a matter of choice, based on how you want your final program to look.

While many programmers just display their comments, others go further, adding lines and positioning their comments in an attempt to make their code *look* nice, as shown here:

```
(****************************************************
*                                                 *
* Function to determine a big number              *
*                                                 *
* This function returns a number that is all the  *
* numbers equal to or less than i, multiplied     *
* together. For instance, if i=3, then this       *
* function will return 1*2*3, or 6.               *
*                                                 *
* Input:     The base number, i                   *
* Output:    The big number                       *
****************************************************)
```

```
Function BigNumber( i : Integer ) : Integer;
VAR
   big : Integer;
BEGIN
   big := 1;                     (* start out with 1 *)

   (*
      - - - - - - - - - - - - - - - - - - - - - - - - - - - - - - - - -
      Multiply for each number. Skip 1 since
      multiplying by 1 doesn't change the
      result.
      - - - - - - - - - - - - - - - - - - - - - - - - - - - - - - - - -
   *)
   FOR count := 2 TO i DO
      big := big * count;
   END;
   RETURN big;              (* send the number back *)

END;                                  (* function *)
```

While this style of programming may appeal to you from a pictorial viewpoint, remember that consistency is the rule—and drawing pretty boxes often takes a good deal of time, especially if you have several dozen (or several hundred!) functions to comment. In addition, including these extra characters in your source files will create more work for the compiler, possibly increasing the time required to build your programs.

tip: *Comments that are aligned are very easy to read—an important consideration for maintaining (making changes to) your code in the future. Just remember that art work takes a lot of time and is best saved for the final version of your program, when no other changes are needed.*

Selecting Variable Names

As you'll recall from Chapter 2, variables are data storage locations within your programs. You should name them in a way that will be simple to recall as you continue programming. Several ideas for naming variables are described in this section. The choice of styles for naming your variables is up to you, but do remember to be consistent.

Assign your variables long enough names that you'll be able to remember easily what each one is used for, but not so long that you dread typing them in for each statement. For instance, there is no need to call variables **i**, **p**, and **t** when you could call them **interest, payment**, and **total**. On the other hand, longer names such as **interest_rate_for_the_loan, payment_for_the_loan**, and **total_amount_paid_on_the_loan** would be tedious to type over and over, and unnecessary for most programs.

There will always be exceptions when you need a very long or very short variable name. Most compilers limit the length of variables to 32 significant characters.

Computer Lingo	
ignificant characters are those characters at the beginning of a variable name that are actually used by the compiler. For instance, your compiler may allow	32 significant characters. This will not stop you from naming a variable with a 60-character name; the compiler will just ignore the last 28 characters.

Capitalization is only significant if the language you use is a *case-sensitive* language (like C, C++, and Modula-2). Variables named **aVariable, avariable**, and **AVARIABLE** would not mean the same thing in a case-sensitive language. For other languages (like BASIC, FORTRAN, COBOL, and Pascal), the case of the variable name does not matter. In any of these languages, **aVariable, avariable**, and **AVARIABLE** would all represent the same variable to the compiler.

Listed here are some common options for capitalization:

Convention	Examples
All lowercase	interestrate paymentamt lastamtdue
All uppercase	INTERESTRATE PAYMENTAMT LASTAMTDUE
First letter capitalized	Interestrate Paymentamt Lastamtdue
First letter of each word capitalized	InterestRate PaymentAmt LastAmtDue
Words separated with underscores	interest_rate payment_amt last_amt_due

These conventions are all acceptable, but the last two are more readable than the others, and are the ones seen most often in the code of professional programmers.

tip: *Even if the language you use is not case-sensitive, variable names that include mixed uppercase and lowercase letters will help make your program much easier to read. Look at the examples above, and pick one that suits you. Remember to be consistent!*

There is another popular capitalization convention, used in several advanced programming environments (notably in the C and C++ programming of Microsoft Windows). *Hungarian Notation* requires that you put an abbreviation of the data type in lowercase letters at the beginning of the variable name. The rest of the variable name uses mixed uppercase and lowercase letters for readability. Here are some examples:

Variable Name	Data Type	What it Might Mean
iLoanTerm	integer	Loan term in years
fPayment	floating point	Payment

Hungarian Notation is only mentioned here to give you a bit of background and understanding. When you read code samples from the latest programming books and magazines, you may see this style in use. In general, it is not recommended for the beginning programmer because it is more difficult to read and understand than the more commonly used conventions listed earlier.

Once you have mastered the more important aspects of programming, you might use Hungarian notation to provide superior documentation within your programs. It is especially appropriate for larger programs, particularly when several programmers are working together. In addition, much of the code written for Microsoft Windows follows Hungarian Notation.

Declaring Variables and Constants

In Chapter 2, you learned about different types of data that can be stored in the computer, such as integers, real numbers, and character strings. In this section, you will see how a programmer would define these pieces of data in a program. In order to store data, there must be some mechanism to hold onto the data so that its value is retained as your program runs. One of these mechanisms is the variable, which is used to store data that can be changed (or varied) during the program. Another is the constant, used to store any value that cannot be changed in the program.

Before a variable can be used to hold data, it must be *declared*. A declaration includes both the variable name and its data type. When the variable is declared, the computer puts some memory aside specifically for the use of that variable. The specific location in memory is usually not important; your program uses the variable's name to tell the computer where to look. In the next sections, you will see examples of how this works.

Standard Data Types

Standard data types are the variables that are available in almost every programming language. They include the types of data required in even the most basic processing: integers, floating point numbers, characters, and strings. Another type of data, supported in some fashion for most languages, is represented by Boolean, or logical, variables. These are variables with TRUE and FALSE values.

Most programming languages support the standard data types. Many also provide a facility that allows you to define your own data types. As you will recall from Chapter 2, data types defined by the programmer are often referred to as structured variables. By creating a structured variable, you can store one or more standard variables together in a single named variable, allowing you to manipulate them in your program with minimal effort.

INTEGERS

As explained in Chapter 2, integers are the counting numbers that you use in normal conversation ("I am thirty years old," "It is 25 degrees outside," "You were traveling 75 in a 55-mile-per-hour zone," etc.). These numbers are used very often in programming; for instance, integers are used for counting how many times something happens.

The following example shows variables being declared in Pascal. Notice that the variable name always comes first, followed by a colon, and then the data type. You can declare more than one variable on the same line by placing commas between the variable names and following the entire list with the colon and the data type.

```
{Pascal declaration of Integers}
counter : Integer;
MilesToTheSun, StarsInTheSky : Longint;
age : Shortint;
```

The **LongInt** and **ShortInt** data types shown here are included in most versions of Pascal. **Long** and **short** mean different things to many computers, but generally indicate the size of the number that can be stored (and the resulting amount of computer storage that must be reserved for the variable). For instance, a **ShortInt** might hold numbers that you know won't get too big: an age, number of visits to the doctor, etc. A **LongInt**, on the other hand, is for very large numbers: the number of miles to the sun, or the number of stars in the sky.

In BASIC, you don't always have to declare your variables before you use them. In many BASIC compilers, you can just start using a variable name, and the compiler will realize that it is an integer by the kind of information you try to assign to that variable. Almost all variants of BASIC use special characters, placed at the end of the variable name, to determine the variable's type. Integer variables end with a percent sign (%) with most compilers. So by using the variable name **Age%**, you have declared an integer variable in BASIC, named **Age%**.

Another method of declaration in BASIC, illustrated in the next example, involves the **Dim** statement, which defines the data type and the amount of space that needs to be reserved for your variable. BASIC has an **Integer** data type, as well as the **Long** data type, which works like the **Longint** type in Pascal.

```
REM BASIC Declaration of Integers
Dim Counter As Integer
Dim MilesToTheSun As Long

REM In the next example, I% is automatically
REM an Integer because of the % character
I% = 1
```

In C, the data type comes first, as you can see in the example below. Contrary to the pattern used in Pascal and BASIC, the data type in C is followed by one or more variable names, again separated by commas. C uses the keywords **long** and **short**, preceding the data type, to define a larger or smaller storage space. These work much like the **Longint** and **Shortint** keywords in Pascal.

```
/* C Declarations of Integers */
int counter;
long int MilesToTheSun, stars_in_the_sky;
short int age;
```

Pascal and C also support something called *unsigned* integers. While a normal integer can have either positive or negative values, an unsigned variable can only be positive.

To declare unsigned variables in Pascal, you use **Word** instead of **Integer**, and **Byte** instead of **Shortint**, as shown here (there is not an equivalent unsigned type for **Longint**):

```
(* You cannot have a negative age or distance,
   so unsigned variables make sense here. *)


Byte Age;
Word MilesToMomsHouse;
```

In C, you simply precede your declaration with the keyword **unsigned**, as shown in the following examples:

```
/* You cannot have a negative age or distance,
   so unsigned variables make sense here. */


unsigned int Age;
unsigned long int MilesToTheSun;
```

Notice that C allows the **unsigned** keyword to be used with **int** variables, as well as with **long int** and **short int** variables.

FLOATING POINT OR REAL NUMBERS

Floating point or real numbers, as you'll recall from Chapter 2, are the type of numbers that you deal with in normal financial transactions. They are numbers that have both a whole number part and a fractional part. You might write checks at the grocery store for $55.24, get paid $17.55 per hour, and have 11.5 vacation days left this year. These are all real numbers.

The capacity of a real number is described in three parts: magnitude, accuracy, and precision. The *magnitude* of a number refers to how large (positive) or small (negative) the whole number portion can get. Numbers from −327.0 through −325.0 might be considered small in magnitude, but −32767.00 would be smaller still.

The *accuracy* of a number means how close to 0 the number can get, or how small the number can become while still remaining positive. Therefore, a value of 0.0000001 displays greater accuracy than does 0.001.

The *precision* of the number is judged by the number of places to the right of the decimal point that can be guaranteed accurate. The number representing pi, used for many geometric calculations, can be approximated as 3.1416. However, greater precision is shown in the approximation 3.1415926.

note:

The more accurate and precise your numbers must be, the more detailed your computer's processing must be—and the more memory your program is likely to require.

Pascal, BASIC, and C provide different types of floating point variables to handle numbers of differing types.

In Pascal, for instance, a **Single** might hold numbers that don't need to be all that precise: an hourly wage, etc. A **Double**, on the other hand, is for very precise numbers: the value of pi taken to 100 places, for instance. Use **Real** variables for all the numbers in between. Selecting the right data type helps you not only to maintain accurate numbers, but also to use the minimum amount of memory for any function. A **Single** takes less space than a **Real**, which, in turn, takes less space than a **Double**.

```
{Pascal declaration of Real Numbers}
hourlyRate : single;
temperature : real;
pi : double;
```

BASIC provides **Single** and **Double** variables for storing real numbers. These are noted with the characters ! and #, respectively, on variable names not defined with **Dim** statements. As with Pascal, **Single** and **Double** refer to the precision and accuracy of the numbers that will be stored, as well as the amount of computer memory that will be required.

```
REM BASIC Declaration of Real Numbers
Dim HourlyRate As Single
Dim OilPressure As Double

REM Alternate definitions, using special
REM characters in the variable names.
HourlyRate! = 12.50
OilPressure# = 3.4655732
```

In C, the three types of floating point variables are **float**, **double**, and **long double**, all shown here:

```
/* C Declarations of Floating Point numbers */
float hourly_rate;
double OilPressure;
long double pi;
```

As with Pascal and BASIC, the different data types are used to control the precision and accuracy of the numbers that will be stored, and to minimize the amount of computer memory that will be used. **float** uses the least memory (and also provides the least precision and accuracy), followed by **double**, and then **long double**.

CHARACTERS AND STRINGS

As you will recall from Chapter 2, characters each use one byte (eight bits) of computer memory, and therefore can have the values 0 through 255 (2 to the 8th power). You may recall that the ANSI character set defines these same values! In Appendix A you will see a table of the actual values stored for all the ANSI characters.

Naturally, a programmer can determine when a number should be displayed, and when the character that the number represents should be shown instead.

While a character variable only holds one letter or digit, a string is a sequence of character used to hold names, addresses, etc. A string takes up one byte of computer memory for each character it holds. Typical strings might include:

```
George Jetson
Leaning Tower of Pisa
ABC
```

In Pascal, the data type for holding a single character is called **char**, while the data type for holding a string is called **string** (pretty straightforward!). You must define the length of the string in the declaration, like this:

```
Name : string[20];
Address : string[40];
```

In BASIC, **String** is the data type for individual characters as well as strings. The character **$** is used to denote string variables. A single character is just a string with a length of 1. Here are some examples of BASIC string variables:

```
REM BASIC method using Dim
Dim MyName As String

REM BASIC method using special characters
MyName$ = "John Ribar"
FirstLetter$ = "A"
```

In C, as in Pascal, a single character variable is called a **char**. To manage a string, you must use an *array* of characters. Arrays are collections of items that are all of the same type; they are discussed in detail later in this chapter. For now, here is an example in C specifying the lengths of two arrays of characters:

```
char name[20], address[40];
```

This line of code declares **name** to be an array (or string, in this case) of up to 20 characters, and **address** to be an array of up to 40 characters. Notice that in C the size of an array immediately follows the variable name, not the data type, as you might have expected. This format allows many strings to be declared on the same line (unlike Pascal, in which each string size must be on a separate line).

BOOLEAN AND LOGICAL VARIABLES

As explained in Chapter 2, Boolean (or logical) variables are used to hold TRUE and FALSE values. Some languages have special data types to handle Boolean variables, while others use numbers to represent the values.

In Pascal, the **Boolean** data type is used to declare logical variables. The values TRUE and FALSE can be assigned to these variables. In addition, numbers can be assigned to Boolean variables in some instances. A Boolean variable with a zero value translates to FALSE, and any non-zero Boolean means TRUE.

In BASIC, integers are used to represent Boolean variables; there is no built-in Boolean data type. Some BASIC compilers allow the keywords **TRUE** and **FALSE** to be assigned to integers. In BASIC, the values for TRUE and FALSE vary by compiler and version; the Microsoft Visual BASIC compiler, for example, uses −1 for TRUE, and 0 for FALSE.

Integers are also used to represent Boolean values in C, so there is no built-in Boolean data type. However, no keywords are predefined for TRUE and FALSE values. C follows the same rule that applies in Pascal, namely that a zero value is considered FALSE, and a non-zero value is considered TRUE.

You may notice that all three languages use the value zero to depict FALSE, and some non-zero value to depict TRUE. If you keep this much in mind, you won't need to remember the specifics of the actual value being used to represent TRUE.

Structured Variables

Structured variables, introduced in Chapter 2, are data types that you can create yourself. Structured variables are generally used for maintaining groups of data that would be difficult to maintain singularly. For instance, if you create a mailing list program, you might have ten pieces of information to keep on each person on the list. In Pascal, the declarations for all of these variables might look like this:

```
Name, Street : String;
City, State : String;
ZipCode, Plus4 : Integer;
Phone, Fax : String;
Age : Shortint;
Birthday : Date;
```

You would probably want to group the information into one structured variable, perhaps calling it **Person**.

Structured variables can also appear within other structured variables. Notice that the **Birthday** field has a data type of **Date**. Since most languages don't have a data type of **Date**, you might need to create one. If not, you would end up with this:

```
BirthMonth, BirthDay, BirthYear : Integer;
```

To create a structured data type requires different keywords and techniques in each language. BASIC, in most cases, does not support programmer-defined variables. Defining the **Date** variable, in Pascal and in C, is detailed in the next two examples.

In Pascal, you begin the declaration of a structured variable with the name that you wish to give the new variable. In this example, **Date** is the name we want to use:

```
{Pascal Version}
type
   Date = record
```

```
    Month : Integer;
    Day : Integer;
    Year : Integer;
End;
```

The new variable name is followed by an equal sign and then by the keyword **record**. Next, the specific fields that you want to include in the data type are listed, followed by the keyword **End**. From this point on, you can use the **Date** data type to declare variables, just as you would use **Integer** or **String**.

In C, you begin the declaration of a structured variable with the keyword **struct** (for structure), followed by the name that you wish to give the new data type (again, **Date** in this case):

```
/* C version */
struct Date
{
    int month;
    int day;
    int year
};
```

The variable name is followed by an opening brace: {. The specific fields that you want to include in the data type are listed next, followed by a closing brace: }. From this point on, you can declare variables of the **Date** type.

remember:

Once you have defined a structured variable, it can be used in your programs just like any other data type.

Notice that in both C and Pascal, a special keyword is used to begin the definition: **struct** in C, and **record** in Pascal. Then, a series of variables and their data types is given; these variables are the elements of your new structured variable.

Arrays

Like structured variables, arrays are groups of information. But instead of being a collection of different kinds of information, an array is a collection of similar items. For instance, in C a string is an array (or group) of characters.

An array can be thought of as a list of items that are all of the same type. An array of test scores, for example, might be used for each student in a classroom. The declaration of such an array, assuming 22 children in the class, might look like one of these examples:

```
Pascal:      scores : Array [1..22] of Integer;

BASIC:       Dim scores(22)

C:           int scores[21];
```

These all declare storage space for 22 test scores. To use the array variables, you now need to specify which of the array elements you are interested in. Here is how you would assign a test score of 85 to the 15th student:

```
{Pascal}
scores[15] := 85;

REM BASIC
scores(15) = 85

/* C */
scores[14] = 85;
```

You may notice that the C example uses the number 14, not 15! This is because, unlike Pascal and BASIC, C always starts counting from 0, not 1. So the array locations in C are from 0 through 21, while Pascal and BASIC use locations 1 through 22. Don't worry; if you start programming in C (or C++), you will get used to this quickly. In Pascal, you can even make the array act like a C array by defining it in this way:

```
{Pascal}
scores : Array [0..21] of Integer;
```

Performing Calculations

Pascal, C, and BASIC (and most other programming languages) all use similar methods for assigning values to variables and using them in mathematical calculations. Luckily, this is all very similar to the basic math skills you learned in school. The examples in this section show the declaration, assignment, and use of variables.

In the following Pascal example, values are assigned to the integers in an array; then these values are totaled. Finally, this total is divided by the number of items in the array, resulting in an average.

```
{Pascal}
VAR {this is the start of variable declarations}
  a : array[1..5] of integer;
  total : integer;
  average : real;
BEGIN
  total := 0;    {assign a value of 0 to total}

  {Now, assign values for array}
  a[1] := 10;
  a[2] := 8;
  a[3] := 15;
  a[4] := 22;
  a[5] := 30;

  {Finally, add them all up, and find average}
  total := a[1] + a[2] + a[3] + a[4] + a[5];
  average := total / 5.0; {Use 5.0 since a real
                   answer is desired. Using 5
               would give an integer result,
                 even though "average" is
               defined as a real variable.}
END;
```

This next example, written in BASIC, performs the same calculations: assigning values to the elements in the array, totaling all the numbers, and finally dividing the total by the number of items in the array to calculate an average.

```
REM BASIC Example of arrays

REM This is the start of variable declarations
Dim a(5) as Integer

REM Assign a value of 0 to total%
total% = 0
```

```
REM Now, assign values for array
a(1) = 10
a(2) = 8
a(3) = 15
a(4) = 22
a(5) = 30

REM Finally, add them all up, and find average
total% = a(1) + a(2) + a(3) + a(4) + a(5)
average! = total% / 5.0

REM  Use 5.0 since a real answer is desired.
REM  Using 5 would give an integer result.
```

Finally, here is a program in C that performs the same calculations as the previous two examples. Notice, however, that the elements in the array are numbered from 0 to 4, instead of from 1 to 5 as was done in Pascal and BASIC.

```
/* C */

/* This is the start of variable declarations */
int a[5];
int total;
float average;

main()
{
  total = 0;    /* assign value of 0 to total */

  /* Now, assign values for array */
  a[0] = 10;
  a[1] = 8;
  a[2] = 15;
  a[3] = 22;
  a[4] = 30;

  Finally, add them all up, and find average}*/
  total = a[0] + a[1] + a[2] + a[3] + a[4];
  average = total / 5.0; /* Use 5.0 since a real
                    answer is desired. Using 5
                would give an integer result. */

}
```

remember: *C always begins counting with 0, not with 1!*

The sample programs in this chapter probably include processes that you are not yet familiar with. For now, just look at the manipulation of the variables (the processes by which assignment, addition, and division take place). You'll learn more about program structure in Chapters 5 and 6.

All three of the preceding examples designate that the array **a** will hold the values 10, 8, 15, 22, and 30. The variable **total** will have the value 85, and the variable **average** will have the value 17.0. (Notice that this is a floating point number, as specified in the declaration of the **average** variable.)

Some languages use the same symbol for assigning a value and for later checking the value. The following BASIC example shows this concept:

```
' First assign a value to the variable
Age% = 32

' Now check for the value
IF Age% = 32 THEN
    PRINT "You are as old as I am!"
END IF
```

However, many languages use different symbols for these two functions. In Pascal and Modula-2, you use the := symbol for assignments, and the = symbol for equality.

```
(*
    Pascal program to show the symbols used for
    assignment and equality.
*)

Program TwoSymbols;

Uses CRT;

VAR
    i : Integer;

BEGIN
    (* First assign a value to the variable *)
    i := 32;
```

```
(* Now check for the value *)
IF i = 32 THEN
    Writeln("You are as old as I am");

END (* program *)
```

C and C++ use a similar concept, utilizing = for assignment and == for equality, as shown in this example:

```
/*
   C program to show the symbols used for
   assignment and equality
*/

#include <stdio.h>    /* allow input and output */

main()
{
   int i;

   /* First assign a value to the variable */
   i = 32;

   /* Now check for the value */
   if (i == 32)
       printf("You are as old as I am \n");

}
```

Storing and Retrieving Data

In the previous example, you saw that variables can receive values and then be used in calculations, creating answers which can then be placed into other variables. However, this type of program is not very useful if it must be rewritten each time you need to use it. After all, what good is a calculator program that has to use the same numbers each time?

The flaw in the example program was that once the total and average were calculated, there was no process for informing the operator of the answers. This section will describe how data can be entered into a program and then displayed for the user.

There are two standard sources for input, and three standard output destinations. Input can be read from the keyboard, or from a file on the disk. Output can be sent to the screen, to the printer, or to a disk file. Files are locations where data can be stored for later use; they reside on one or more of the computer's disk drives. In most programming languages, the commands that perform input and output are similar for all sources and destinations.

Keyboard Input

Many programs are designed so that the user of the program can enter certain information into the program directly from the computer keyboard. This information is the user's *input* to the program. As the programmer, you need to provide a method of getting this information into your programs. Luckily, most computer languages provide commands for handling input.

In Pascal, the **Read()** procedure is used to read information from the user. **Read()** will read a value for a variable. The data type that you specify tells the procedure what type of data it will be reading. For example, the following example would cause **Read()** to expect an integer value from the user.

```
{Pascal}

var
   aVal : Integer;

   Read(aVal);   {looks for an integer}
```

note: *For now, think of procedures as special commands that are available while you are programming. To differentiate them from the commands that are built into each language, procedure names are denoted with parentheses, as in **Read()**. In Chapter 6, you will learn more about procedures and discover how to create your own.*

BASIC works the same way that Pascal does, in that the data type indicates what kind of information can be expected. The **Input** command is used for receiving information from the user of your program. So in the following example, a single-precision real number should be entered by the user:

```
Input Rate!
Print "Your pay rate is ", Rate!
```

remember: *In BASIC, when the* **!** *character is included in a variable, it indicates that the variable will be a single-precision real number.*

In C, the type of information to be input must be specified by the programmer as part of the procedure itself. The **scanf()** procedure is used to scan the keyboard for information from the user. The **scanf()** procedure takes two parameters—the format of the data to be input, and the variable (or variables) into which the data should be placed.

Computer Lingo

The values that are given to a procedure when it starts are called *parameters*. These are used by the processing that occurs within the procedure. Parameters may be used to control how a procedure runs, or to specify values upon which the procedure will function.

The use of **scanf()** in C also involves *pointers,* which are simply devices used by C to change variable values in memory. The **&** symbol in the following example is sending the actual physical memory address of the variable into the **scanf()** procedure; this will allow **scanf()** to place the information (the integer value read from the user) into a known storage location.

```
int inVal;

scanf(" %d", &inVal);
```

This kind of memory location manipulation is not available (and not necessary) in most languages. This feature is one of the ways in which C is more powerful, and more confusing to the beginning programmer; without using the **&** symbol, **inVal** would not receive a new value!

The **%d** in **scanf()** denotes that a decimal number is expected. C uses data *specifiers,* such as **%d**, for both input and output. These specifiers give **scanf()** and **printf()** (the output procedure) a great deal of flexibility. There are dozens of specifiers available in C (and in C++). They cover all of the standard data types, as well as the use of integers in octal and hexadecimal format. In addition, the specifiers may define the format of the number (including the number of decimal places, the minimum width of the field that will be used, whether the information will be left-justified or right-justified, and whether a numeric field should be zero-filled).

Screen and Printer Output

Just as it is important to get information into your program, it is also important to get the final results back out of the program to the user.

The procedures that Pascal, BASIC, and C use for receiving input are similar to those used for producing output. Pascal uses **Write()** and **WriteLn()**, BASIC uses **PRINT**, and C uses **printf()**.

The Pascal **Write()** procedure outputs the value of the variable to the screen, and then remains on the same line as the output value. **WriteLn()** performs the same function, but inserts a carriage return when the printing is finished, moving down to the next line. The following example illustrates this process:

```
{Pascal example of Input and Output}
Program IO;

VAR
    firstName, lastName : String[15];
    age : integer;

BEGIN

    Read(firstName);
    Read(lastName);
    Read(age);

    Write('Hello ');
    Write(firstName);
    Write(' ');
    WriteLn(lastName);
    WriteLn('It is nice to see you!');
    Write('You are ');
    Write(age*12);
    WriteLn(' months old.');

END {program}
```

If a user entered the name *Bill Smith* into this program, along with an age of *20,* the following lines would be output:

```
Hello Bill Smith
It is nice to see you!
You are 240 months old.
```

You see that the program does not go to the next line until a **WriteLn()** is used, rather than a regular **Write()**. Also, notice that the **Write()** and **WriteLn()** procedures can output variables, the results of calculations, or actual text or numeric data.

BASIC uses the **PRINT** statement to output information on the screen, a variation of the **PRINT** statement to write information to files, and the **LPRINT** statement to write to the printer. All three statements have the same general form.

The following example shows BASIC statements that will read information from the user, perform a calculation, and then print the results to the screen and to the printer.

```
REM BASIC Example of Input and Output

PRINT "What is your name?"
INPUT Name$
PRINT "How old are you (in years)?"
INPUT Age%

REM Determine number of months old
Age% = Age% * 12

PRINT "Well, ", Name$, ", you are ";
PRINT Age%, " months old"

REM Now put the information on the printer
LPRINT Name$, " is ", Age%, " months old"
```

Notice that the **PRINT** statement allows you to put both variables and text (enclosed in quotation marks) on the same line. Also, if a **PRINT** line ends with a semicolon (as does the third **PRINT** line above), the program will continue to print on the same line. Otherwise, the program will move to the next line at the end of a **PRINT** statement, (as with the **WriteLn()** procedure in Pascal).

C uses the **printf()** procedure (for *print* formatted) to show things on the screen, and the **fprintf()** (file version *print* formatted) to write to the printer or to a file. The first parameter that you provide with **fprintf()** indicates the destination; it is followed by the format and data parameters used with **printf()**.

Remember that **printf()** expects a format, and then the data to be printed. The format can include actual text to be printed, as well as the specifiers that show where and how to print variable values. The BASIC example above is rewritten here in C.

```
/* C example of Input and Output */

main()
{
    char Name[20];
    int Age;

    printf("What is your name? ");
    scanf(" %s", Name);
    printf("How old are you (in years)?");
    scanf(" %d", &Age);

    /* Determine number of months old */
    Age = Age*12;

    printf("Well, %s, you are ", Name);
    printf("%d months old \n", Age );

    /* Now put the information on the printer */
    fprintf( stdprn, "%s is %d months old \n",
        Name, Age );

}
```

There are a few things you should notice in this example. First, C uses the characters **\n** to tell **printf()** when to start a new line. These characters are included in the format parameter to **printf()**. Also, the keyword **stdprn** is a designation for the standard printer; other values for this parameter include **stdout** (which outputs to the screen) or **stdaux** (which outputs to the communications port). In addition, actual disk file identifiers can be used here.

Streamlining the Process

Now that you can create and manipulate several types of variables, controlling the flow of a program becomes very important. Imagine writing a program to calculate and print 500 payroll checks, all identical in the layout of the employee name and address, amount of pay, etc. You would certainly want to avoid writing the same sequence of statements 500 times!

Flow control statements control the order in which the program statements will be executed. With a flow control statement that allowed looping, for instance, the processing statement of the payroll program would be written only once, and then executed for each of the 500 employees. In Chapter 5, you will see how this is done.

Chapter 5

Controlling the Flow

C H A P T E R 4 briefly discussed a program that might be written to calculate and print 500 similar payroll checks. The following example shows an abbreviated version of just such a program.

Examine the program closely, however, and you will notice that it has a rather burdensome design:

```
(* Pascal check-writing program *)
program Checks;

Uses CRT;

VAR
    amt : Real;
    name : String;

BEGIN
    Write("Enter amount for check 1: ");
    Readln(amt);
    Write("Enter payee name: ");
    Readln(name);
    { now process the check ... }

    Write("Enter amount for check 2: ");
    Readln(amt);
    Write("Enter payee name: ");
    Readln(name);
    { now process the check ... }

    Write("Enter amount for check 3: ");
    Readln(amt);
    Write("Enter payee name: ");
    Readln(name);
    { now process the check ... }
```

```
(**** etcetera, etcetera, etcetera ****)

    Write("Enter amount for check 500: ");
    Readln(amt);
    Write("Enter payee name: ");
    Readln(name);
    { now process the check ... }
END
```

If this program were printed in its entirety, it would be many pages long! This is because the unfortunate person writing such a program would have entered the same sequence of statements 500 times over.

Obviously, there must be a better way. In fact, these kinds of repetitive chores are what computers were designed to take care of—leaving human beings free to tackle more creative tasks.

To streamline your work as a programmer, you need to learn how to use flow control statements. As mentioned in Chapter 4, flow control statements allow programmers to control the order in which the program statements will be executed. With a flow control statement that allows looping, such as the one shown in the next example, the processing statements in the payroll program would only have to be written once. They could then be executed for each of the 500 employees.

Computer Lingo

When a program instructs the computer to repeat a piece of code multiple times, the process is referred to as *looping*. A *loop* can consist of one statement or a large group of statements. Some loops are repeated a specific number of times, while others are repeated until a specific condition is met. Be careful when you specify the *exit condition* (the condition that makes the loop end), or you may create an *infinite loop*; these loops continue forever, locking up your computer and generally requiring you to reboot!

```
(* Pascal check-writing program *)
program Checks2;

Uses CRT;
```

```
VAR
    amt : Real;
    name : String;
    count : Integer;

BEGIN

    FOR count := 1 TO 500 DO
    BEGIN
        Write("Enter amount for check ");
        Write(count);
        Write(": ");   {so it looks nice}
        Readln(amt);
        Write("Enter payee name: ");
        Readln(name);
        { now process the check ... }
    END;

END
```

This chapter will introduce the concept of a block of code, and then describe two main types of flow control statements. The first type is used to make a decision and then run selected code, according to the results. The second type is used to repeat sections of code multiple times, in a controlled manner.

note: *Although the examples in this chapter are written in C, Pascal, and BASIC, rest assured that other languages employ these same concepts. Every language has some sort of **IF...THEN...ELSE** statements, and at least one of the looping methods shown here. If you grasp these concepts, using them with other languages will come naturally.*

Program Blocks

In some programming languages, such as Pascal and C, a group of statements executed together is known as a *block*. As you may recall from Chapter 4, a block of statements in the C language is surrounded by braces, { and }, while in Pascal the block is surrounded by the keywords **BEGIN** and **END**. This concept is very important when you are dealing with program flow.

When a control statement makes a decision, either a single line of code will be executed, or a block will be executed. For instance, in the listing below, one of two **printf()** statements is executed, based on the outcome of the **if** statement. (**if** statements are covered in the next section.)

```
/*
   C Program to demonstrate if statements
*/
#include <stdio.h>

main()
{
    int a;    /* define the variable */

    printf("Enter an integer value: ");
    scanf(" %d", &a);    /* read value from the user */

    if (a==1)    /* check the value of a */
        printf("a is one\n");
    else
        printf("a is not one\n");
}
```

In the next listing, a series of commands should be executed together. They are placed within braces and executed as a block.

```
/*
   C Program to demonstrate blocks
*/
#include <stdio.h>

main()
{
    int c, d;              /* declare some variables */

    printf("Please enter 1 or 2: ");
    scanf(" %d", &c );    /* get a value from the user */

    if (c==2)             /* check the value of c */
    {
        d = 2;
        printf("Everything is now 2\n");
    }
    else
    {
```

```
        d = 3;
        printf("Nothing is 2 now! c is %d and d is %d\n",
               c, d);
    }
}
```

tip:

You may notice that the code between the braces is indented. Although this indentation is not necessary, it is a good practice. Indenting makes the code more readable because it better delineates the block as a cohesive unit of code. This is true for most languages, but especially for Pascal, C, and C++. For a more detailed discussion of indentation, refer back to Chapter 4.

In Pascal, the concept is similar. If only one statement is to be executed following a decision, it can be used directly. But if multiple statements are to be executed, the **BEGIN** and **END** delimiters must be used, as shown in this example:

```
{
    Pascal Program to demonstrate blocks
}
program Blocks;

uses CRT;    (* allow for screen input/output *)

VAR
    Age, YearsToGo : Integer;

BEGIN {starts the program}

    Write("How old are you? ");
    Readln(Age);

    IF Age < 22 THEN

        Writeln("You are still a young pup!");

    ELSE BEGIN {starts the block}
        Writeln("You are now an adult");
        YearsToGo := 55 - Age;
        Write("You only have ");
        Write(YearsToGo);
        Writeln(" years until retirement!");
```

```
    END; {ends the block}

END {ends the program}
```

BASIC does not use the concept of blocks the same way that Pascal does. In BASIC, each control statement starts its own block, and **END** statements complete each block. An **IF** statement is shown in the following example:

```
IF A>B THEN
    PRINT "A is greater than B"
END
```

In BASIC, the format of the **IF** statement does not change, whether one or many target statements are executed.

Now that you have seen several examples of blocks, and how they are used with **IF...THEN...ELSE** statements, you should learn about the decision-making statements themselves.

Making Decisions

The first type of control statements are those used when a decision is necessary. An **IF** statement checks the value of a Boolean variable, or an equation with a Boolean answer. If the value is TRUE, specific code is executed. If the value is FALSE, then no code is executed, unless there is an **ELSE** clause. An **ELSE** clause is used to specify an alternate course of events—something that the program should do if the condition in the **IF** statement is false. In the above examples, if the original condition is false, the code following **ELSE** is executed.

A **switch** or **CASE** statement (depending on the language you are using) will first check the value of a specified variable and then, depending on that value, jump to a specific section of code. The C language uses the **switch** statement for this purpose, while Pascal and BASIC use the **CASE** statement.

IF...THEN...ELSE Statements

An **IF** statement is used when there is a decision to be made that will effect whether certain lines of code should be executed. It has several forms, which are discussed here.

THE **IF** STATEMENT WITH A SINGLE TARGET STATEMENT

In this form of the **IF** statement, there is no **ELSE** clause, and only a single target statement needs to be executed if the condition is true.

```
C:      if (condition)
            statement 1;
```

```
Pascal:  IF condition THEN
            statement 1;
```

```
BASIC:   IF condition THEN statement 1
```

THE **IF** STATEMENT WITH MULTIPLE TARGET STATEMENTS

In this form of the **IF** statement, there is no **ELSE** clause, but there are multiple target statements to be performed if the condition is true.

```
C:      if (condition)
        {
          statement 1;
          statement 2;
          /* could be more statements here */
        }
```

```
Pascal:  IF condition THEN
         BEGIN
           statement 1;
           statement 2;
           { could be more statements here }
         END;
```

```
BASIC:   IF condition THEN
            statement 1
            statement 2
         END IF
```

THE IF...ELSE STATEMENT WITH ALTERNATIVE TARGET STATEMENTS

In this form of **IF** statement, an **ELSE** clause is used. This provides an alternative set of instructions, in case the condition is false.

```
C:      if (condition)
        {
            statement1;
            statement2;
        }
        else
        {
            other_statement1;
            other_statement2;
        }
```

```
Pascal:  IF condition THEN
         BEGIN
             statement1;
             statement2;
         END
         ELSE
         BEGIN
             other_statement1;
             other_statement2;
         END;
```

```
BASIC:   IF condition THEN
             statement1
             statement2
         ELSE
             other_statement1
             other_statement2
         END IF
```

Each of the blocks in these examples consists of two statements. Keep in mind, however, that a block can include any number of statements, including none!

remember: *In C, blocks of code are surrounded by braces; in Pascal, they are surrounded by the keywords* ***BEGIN*** *and* ***END***.

MORE ON THE **IF** STATEMENT

The **IF** statement is composed of a condition and one or more target statements. The condition is always surrounded by parentheses in C, as shown in the above example. In Pascal and BASIC, the condition is always followed by the keyword **THEN**.

If only one target statement needs to be executed, based on the result of the condition, then the block delimiters are not required. Otherwise, a standard block is used. For stylistic considerations (in other words, to make your program as easy to read as possible), the target statement or block should be indented from the **IF** and **ELSE** statements.

The **ELSE** portion of the statement is optional. It is used when there is an alternative set of code to be executed if the original condition is not true.

The condition portion of the statement is any variable, statement, or equation that returns a value. This can include a test for equality or inequality, the name of a Boolean variable, or a call to any other type of statement that returns a Boolean value.

In C, these options are somewhat expanded. C does not have an actual Boolean data type. Thus, it regards any integer with a value of zero to be FALSE; any other value is considered to be TRUE. The next example will illustrate how this works.

caution: *The condition part of an* ***if*** *statement is where many beginning C programmers have the most problems. In C,* == *is used to compare values, and* = *is for assignment. However,* ***(a=10)*** *is a valid condition statement; it assigns* ***a*** *the value of 10, and returns that value* ***(10)***. *The condition is therefore true, because it returns a non-zero value. Be aware, however, that* ***(a==10)*** *is also a valid condition statement; if* ***a*** *is equal to 10, a value of TRUE (a non-zero value) is returned; otherwise FALSE (zero) is returned. Be careful that you use the right operation in your* ***if*** *statements.*

```
/*
    C program to show if conditions
*/
#include <stdio.h>

main()
```

```
            {
                int a, b;

                a = 0;

                printf("Enter a value for a: ");
                scanf(" %d", &a);
                if (a == 0)
                    printf("a is zero \n");
                else
                {
                    printf("a is ");
                    b = a % 2;   /* Find out if it is odd or even,
                                    by using the modulus operation.
                                    If it is odd, the result is 1;
                                    if even, the result is 0. */

                if (b) /* if non-zero value ... */
                        printf("odd\n");
                    else
                        printf("even\n");
                }


            }
```

A numeric comparison → (pointing to `if (a == 0)`)

A Boolean comparison → (pointing to `if (b) /* if non-zero value ... */`)

If the condition yields a TRUE value, the statement or block immediately following it is executed. If there is an **else** option, it is executed only if the original condition is found to be false. If there is not an **else** option, and the **if** condition fails, nothing will be executed.

You may notice two statements in the above C and Pascal examples that do not seem to make sense. In C, the following statement is a special command to the compiler:

```
#include <stdio.h>
```

This command is used to include the contents of **stdio.h** (the *ST*an*D*ard *I*nput and *O*utput *H*eader file) in your program. Establishing access to this header file allows you to use **printf()**, **scanf()**, and a multitude of similar procedures.

In C, the **include** command lets you include the contents of specific files in your program. These files describe the functions and data types that are available to your program. Most C compilers come with several of these header files;

each of the header files describe some of the functions available in the C run-time library, which is added to each of your programs automatically by the compiler.

In Pascal, the **Uses** command performs a function similar to that of the C **include** command. The following statement

```
Uses CRT;
```

tells the Pascal compiler that your program uses the CRT library, which is a set of additional Pascal functions and procedures.

There are many libraries and header files available in both C and Pascal. The commands shown here represent the most common use of these library procedures, since **input** and **output** are found in almost every program.

Now look at the following Pascal example, paying special attention to the simple **IF** statement located near the end of the program.

```
{
    Pascal program to demonstrate IF statements
}
program OnlyIf;

uses CRT;      (* allow for screen input/output *)

VAR
    month : Integer;

BEGIN

    Write("Enter a month number (1-12): ");
    Readln(month);

    IF month = 1 THEN
        Writeln("This is January");

END
```

This program shows an **IF** statement with a single target statement. If the variable **month** has a value of 1, then the **Write()** statement will be executed. But what happens if **month** is 2? In this example, nothing will happen. However, a slight change will broaden the possibilities, as shown in the next example:

```
{
    Pascal program to print whether the given
    month is January
}
program IfElse;

uses CRT;      (* allow for screen input/output *)

VAR
    month : Integer;    { declare the variable }

BEGIN {main program}

    Write("Enter a month number (1-12): ");
    Readln(month);

    IF month = 1 THEN
       Writeln("This is January");
    ELSE
       Writeln("This is not January");

END {main program}
```

Now the program demonstrates the use of an **ELSE** statement to specify an alternative result. This process can be extended even further; an **ELSE** statement can contain another **IF** statement. Examine the next listing to see how **IF** and **ELSE** statements can be strung together.

```
{
    Pascal program with lots of IFs and ELSEs
}
program ManyIfs;

uses CRT;      (* allow for screen input/output *)

VAR
    month : Integer;    { declare the variable }

BEGIN {main program}

    Write("Enter a month number (1-12): ");
    Readln(month);

    { now check for the correct month! }
```

```
        IF month = 1 THEN
           Writeln("This is January");
        ELSE IF month = 2 THEN
           Writeln("This is February");
        ELSE IF month = 3 THEN
           Writeln("This is March");
        ELSE IF month = 4 THEN
           Writeln("This is April");
        ELSE IF month = 5 THEN
           Writeln("This is May");
        ELSE IF month = 6 THEN
           Writeln("This is June");
        ELSE IF month = 7 THEN
           Writeln("This is July");
        ELSE IF month = 8 THEN
           Writeln("This is August");
        ELSE IF month = 9 THEN
           Writeln("This is September");
        ELSE IF month = 10 THEN
           Writeln("This is October");
        ELSE IF month = 11 THEN
           Writeln("This is November");
        ELSE IF month > 12 THEN
        BEGIN
           Write("This is NOT a month! ");
           Writeln("You should use 1 thru 12");
        END
        ELSE
           Writeln("This must be December!");

END {main program}
```

Unfortunately, multiple combinations of **IF** and **ELSE** statements can become very complicated, and difficult to read. You can alleviate this problem by using a **switch** or **CASE** statement to indicate various possible conditions and their corresponding results.

Selection Statements: **switch**, **CASE**, and **SELECT CASE**

Selection statements are similar to **IF** statements that have lots of **ELSE** clauses. However, when a selection statement is used, the result is a more readable piece of code. You will see this in the next three examples, each of which performs a similar function to that of the preceding example, but which replaces the string of **IF...ELSE** statements with a selection statement.

The first example shows the use of a C **switch** statement. This is a special statement that acts like a train switching yard; the path your program takes is controlled by the information given to the switch.

```c
/*
   C program to show if and switch statements
*/
#include <stdio.h>   /* allow for screen input/output */

main()
{
    int month;            /* declare an integer variable */
    printf("Enter the month: ");      /* ask for input */
    scanf(" %d", &month );           /* get the input */
    if (month < 1)        /* check for invalid inputs */
        printf("That month is too small!\n");
    else if (month > 12)
    {
        printf("That month is too big.\n");
        month = 12;       /* put user in holiday spirit! */
    }

    switch (month)              /* check for actual value */
    {
        case 1:
        case 2:
            printf("Boy, is it cold out!\n");
            break;
        case 12:
            printf("Happy Holidays!\n");
            break;
        case 3:
        case 4:
        case 5:
            printf("Time to plant your garden.\n");
            break;
        case 6:
        case 7:
        case 8:
            printf("Let's go out to the ball game.\n");
            break;
```

```
   case 9:
   case 10:
   case 11:
      printf("Time to harvest the vegetables.\n");
      break;
   default:
      printf("I do not know what to say!\n");
      break    };                      /* end of switch statement */
}
```

In the preceding example, a number representing a month is input by the user of the program. Depending on the month selected, one of six text statements is printed. If the month is 1 (January) or 2 (February), the program mentions the weather; if the month is 12 (December), a holiday greeting is printed. Other months induce different responses. Notice the **default** clause at the end of the program; this is used when the number entered does not match any of the values (1–12) specified in the program. The invalid number does not represent any month, so the program prints an appropriate message ("I do not know what to say!").

In the next listing, a Pascal **CASE** statement is used to perform the same function:

```
(*
   Pascal program to show IF and CASE statements
*)
program CaseDemo;

uses CRT;                   (* allow for screen input/output *)

VAR
   month : INTEGER;         (* declare an integer variable *)
BEGIN
   Write('Enter the month: ');          (* ask for input *)
   ReadLn( month );                      (* get the input *)
   IF month < 1 THEN          (* check for invalid inputs *)
      WriteLn('That month is too small!')
   ELSE IF month > 12 THEN
   BEGIN
      WriteLn('That month is too big.\n');
      month := 12;            (* put user in holiday spirit! *)
   END;
```

```
CASE month OF                   (* check for actual value *)
   1, 2:              WriteLn('Boy, is it cold out!');
   12:
     WriteLn('Happy Holidays!');


   3..5:
     WriteLn('Time to plant your garden.');
   6..8:
     WriteLn('Let's go out to the ball game.');
   9..11:
     WriteLn('Time to harvest the vegetables.');
   ELSE
     WriteLn('I do not know what to say!');
   END;                         (* end of CASE statement *)
END
```

In this program, as in the C example, a number representing a month is input by the user of the program. Then one of six text statements is printed, based on the number that was entered. The **ELSE** clause at the end of the program serves the same purpose as the **default** clause in the preceding example. When the number entered does not match any of the values specified in the program, it does not represent a month at all, so "I do not know what to say!" is printed.

Notice that, unlike the C language, Pascal allows a range of values to be listed in each case:

```
6..8:
        WriteLn('Let's go out to the ball game.');
```

In the Pascal example, 6..8 is used to select the months 6, 7, or 8. Here is the corresponding C code:

```
case 6:
case 7:
case 8:
        printf("Let's go out to the ball game.\n");
        break;
```

As you can see, the C code here is a bit more lengthy and repetitive, because C requires a separate case for each possible value.

The third example shows the use of a BASIC **SELECT CASE** statement. In BASIC, your program will select the group of **CASE** statements that will be executed, based on the value given to the **SELECT CASE** statement.

```
'    BASIC program to show IF and SELECT CASE

PRINT "Enter the month: ";
INPUT month%
IF month% < 1 THEN
    PRINT "That month is too small."
ELSEIF month% > 12 THEN
    PRINT "That month is too big"
    month% = 12
END IF
```

```
SELECT CASE month%
   CASE 1 TO 2
     PRINT "Boy, is it cold out!"
   CASE 12
     PRINT "Happy Holidays"
   CASE 3 TO 5
     PRINT "Time to plant your garden."
   CASE 6 TO 8
     PRINT "Let's go out to the ball game"
   CASE 9 TO 11
     PRINT "Time to harvest the vegetables"
   CASE ELSE
     PRINT "I do not know what to say!"
END SELECT
```

In this program, as in the C and Pascal examples, a number representing a month is entered by the user. Then one of six text statements is printed, based on the input number. Notice that in BASIC, the **CASE ELSE** clause is used when an invalid number is entered, and as in the earlier programs, the message "I do not know what to say!" is printed.

Notice also that, like Pascal, BASIC allows a range of values to be listed in each case. In BASIC, the range looks like this:

```
CASE 6 TO 8
      PRINT "Let's go out to the ball game"
```

The selection statement uses a different type of condition than is used by the **IF** statement. In the three examples above, the **month** variable is being used as the selection condition. Because **month** can hold one of several values, several **CASE** statements are used to specify different results for all the possible values. A special default statement is used to cover all unknown values—the

default clause in C, the **ELSE** clause in Pascal, and the **CASE ELSE** clause in BASIC.

When a selection statement is executed, the **CONDITION** value is checked against the available **CASE** statements. If one matches, the code following that **CASE** statement is executed. If no match is found, the default clause is used.

Using a selection statement is more efficient than using multiple **IF...THEN...ELSE** statements. In the previous examples, the outcome of each **CASE** statement was only a printing statement. In other types of programs, however, there is often the need for many lines of code for each case. In these situations, it can be very confusing to have to thread through many **IF** and **ELSE** statements. Having all the choices organized under a single selection statement will make your programs much simpler to read.

tip:

*When deciding whether to use a group of **IF** statements or a selection statement, consider the nature of the arguments. An **IF** statement can take any equation that returns a value of TRUE or FALSE. In C, this even includes floating point values. A selection statement, on the other hand, is limited to specific (non-fractional) values.*

Once the selection statement has found a matching case, the code beneath the **CASE** statement is executed, and the selection statement ends. In the C language, however, the **switch** statement has a peculiarity that can be a help or a hindrance. When a matching **case** statement is found, the flow of the program jumps to that statement and continues executing code. This means that all the subsequent **case** statements will also be executed, unless a **break** statement is found.

In C, the **break** statement is used within a **case** statement to exit the **switch** statement, jumping over other pieces of code that should not be executed. (This is done automatically in BASIC and Pascal.) Without the **break** statement, all the code following the selected **case** statement is executed. Sometimes this can be a useful option, and it certainly gives you more control. Look at the following example:

```
/*
   C program to show switch statements that fall through
*/
#include <stdio.h>

main()
{
```

```
    int num, add;   /* declare necessary variables */

    num = 5;        /* start with a value of 5 */
    add = 5;        /* we want to increment by 5 */

    switch (add)
    {
       case 5: num += 1;
       case 4: num += 1;
       case 3: num += 1;
       case 2: num += 1;
       case 1: num += 1;
       default : printf("Done adding\n");
    }

    printf("Variable num = %d \n",num);

}
```

As you can see, the value of the **num** variable, 5, will match the first **case** statement, so the code following that statement will be executed. Next, all the other **case** statements will be executed as well, because there is no **break** statement that would cause the program to break out of the **switch** process. The execution of this program will produce the following results:

```
Done adding
Variable num = 10
```

Although this is a rather simple example, it does show you how a **switch** statement will execute when no **break** statement is encountered. If you add **break** statements, as shown below, and run the program again, the outcome will be different.

```
/*
    C program to show switch statement with breaks
*/
#include <stdio.h>

main()
{
    int num, add;   /* declare necessary variables */
```

```
num = 5;        /* start with a value of 5 */
add = 5;        /* we want to increment by 5 */

switch (add)
{
   case 5: num += 1;
           break;
   case 4: num += 1;
           break;
   case 3: num += 1;
           break;
   case 2: num += 1;
           break;
   case 1: num += 1;
           break;
   default : printf("Done adding\n");
}
   printf("Variable num = %d \n",num);

}
```

In this example, as in the first one, the **num** variable will match the first **case** statement, so the code following that statement will be executed. In the very next line, however, the program will encounter the **break** statement. This will cause the program to jump ahead, past the closing bracket at the end of the **switch** statement, and execute the **printf** statement. All of the **case** statements that follow the matching one are now disregarded, so the output of the program changes to:

```
Done adding
Variable num = 6
```

In all of the examples above, the selection conditions have dealt only with integer values. However, character and Boolean values are just as valid. For instance, the following program demonstrates a simple method for checking the response of a user.

```
(*
   Pascal program with a character-based
   CASE statement
*)
program CharCase;
```

```
Uses CRT;

VAR
   ch : Char; (* declare the variable *)

BEGIN {main program}

   Write("Enter a Y (yes) or N (no): ");
   Readln(ch);

   CASE ch OF
      'Y', 'y' :
            Writeln("Thanks for saying Yes");
      'N', 'n' :
            Writeln("So sorry that you said no");
      ELSE
      BEGIN
         Writeln("I see that you are undecided!");
         Writeln("You did not choose Yes or No!");
      END;
   END;

END {main program}
```

This program also demonstrates a principle that you should remember for your own programs: Uppercase and lowercase input values should produce the same results! By using two case values, one each for uppercase and lowercase, you provide for identical handling of both possible inputs. In doing so, you avoid forcing your users to remember whether they have to press a lowercase or an uppercase letter in response to a question.

Repetitive Processing

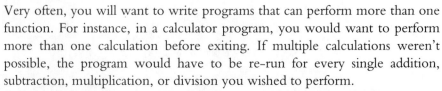

Very often, you will want to write programs that can perform more than one function. For instance, in a calculator program, you would want to perform more than one calculation before exiting. If multiple calculations weren't possible, the program would have to be re-run for every single addition, subtraction, multiplication, or division you wished to perform.

There are also times when a section of code needs to be performed several times. Sometimes, you will know how many times the code should execute when the program is run (printing reports for 12 months, calculating payroll for 20 employees, etc.). In other cases, as with a calculator, you will want the program to keep going until the user decides to quit.

In computer programming, repetitive processing tasks can be simplified with the use of loops. Among the popular languages available today, **FOR**, **WHILE**, and **REPEAT** loops are most common.

FOR Loops

A **FOR** loop is used to execute a target statement or block multiple times. To use a **FOR** loop, you use an *index variable*. This variable keeps track of how many times the loop has been run. In constructing a **FOR** loop, you first initialize the variable, and then set a limit that will cause the program to exit the loop when appropriate.

The general format of the **for** loop in C is shown below. This format only allows for a single statement to be executed each time through the loop.

```
for ( init ; control ; increment )
    statement;
```

The *init*, *control*, and *increment* statements perform special functions within the **for()** statement; they will be discussed later in this chapter.

If more than one target statement needs to be executed in the loop, the following format is used:

```
for ( init ; control ; increment )
{
    statement1;
    statement2;
}
```

In Pascal, the following form is used for **FOR** loops with a single target statement:

```
FOR counter := start TO finish [BY increment] DO
    statement;
```

and the following format is used when multiple target statements are to be executed as the loop continues:

FOR *counter* := *start* TO *finish* [BY *increment*] DO
BEGIN
  statement1;
  statement2;
END;

Normally, Pascal increments the *counter* variable by 1 each time the loop is run. The optional **BY** *increment* clause is used to change the size of the increment.

In BASIC, the format for the **FOR** statement is very similar to the Pascal form. However, the format in BASIC is the same whether a single target statement or multiple target statements will be performed:

FOR *counter* = *start* TO *finish* [STEP *increment*]
  statement; ' one or more statements allowed
NEXT *counter*

In Pascal and BASIC, the use of the **FOR** statement is straightforward. For instance, to print the first ten numbers in Pascal, you could use the following program:

```
(* Pascal FOR loop *)

program Count10;

Uses CRT;

VAR
   c : Integer;

BEGIN
   Writeln("By ones:");
   FOR c := 1 TO 10 DO { One at a time }
     WriteLn(c);

   Writeln(); (* Print a blank line *)
   Writeln("By twos:");
   FOR c := 2 TO 10 BY 2 DO { Count by 2's }
     WriteLn(c);
END
```

If this program were run, the following output would appear:

```
By ones:
1
2
3
4
5
6
7
8
9
10

By twos:
2
4
6
8
10
```

The BASIC **FOR** loop, illustrated in the next example, works essentially the same way as those in Pascal. In BASIC, each time through the loop, the counter variable (**c%** in the listing below) is incremented by one, unless the **STEP** clause has been used to specify another increment.

```
' BASIC FOR Loop

PRINT "By ones:"
FOR c% = 1 TO 10   ' One at a time
    PRINT c%
NEXT c%

PRINT ' print a blank line
PRINT "By twos:"
FOR c% = 2 TO 10 STEP 2 ' Count by 2's
    PRINT c%
NEXT c%
```

As might be expected, the output from this program would look the same as that produced by the preceding Pascal example:

```
By ones:
1
2
3
4
5
6
7
8
9
10

By twos:
2
4
6
8
10
```

The **for** statement is slightly different in C. The concept is the same, but the statement itself is more powerful, requiring a little more explanation. In C, the condition consists of three parts, separated by semicolons. However, all three parts are optional; in fact, the simplest form of the **for** loop is a forever loop:

```
for (;;)
{
    statement_or_block;
}
```

This loop will continue to execute the target code forever, unless a **break** statement is found. (This is a second use for the **break** statement. As you'll recall, the first was with the **switch** statement.) To understand why the loop will keep running, you must understand the three parts of the condition:

```
for ( init ; control ; increment )
    statement_or_block;
```

The *init*, *control*, and *increment* are three separate C-language statements that perform special functions within the **for()** statement.

The initialization statement (*init*) is executed before the loop starts. This part of the condition is usually used to initialize the index variable, or any other variables needed within the loop. If no initialization statement is included in the condition, nothing will be initialized.

The *control* statement is executed before each iteration of the loop. This part of the condition is generally used to limit the number of times the loop will execute. If the control statement has a non-zero value (TRUE), then the loop continues to execute. If the condition does not include a control statement, a value of TRUE is assumed, causing the loop to execute again.

The *increment* statement is executed at the end of each traversal through the loop. This is usually used to increment the index variable. If no statement is entered here, nothing will be executed, and the next test of the control statement will occur. The most common use of the increment statement is to increment the index variable (in this case, **i**), using the C increment operator (**++**), as shown here:

```
i++;
```

You can also perform other operations. If you want to multiply the index variable by 2 each time the loop runs, your condition might look like this:

```
for (i=0; i<100; i=i*2 )
```

A **for** loop is actually a version of a **while** loop. The next two loops are functionally identical:

```
/* the for loop version */

for (i=0; i<10; i++)
   printf("i = %d \n",i);
```

This loop would produce the following output:

```
i = 0
i = 1
i = 2
i = 3
i = 4
i = 5
i = 6
i = 7
i = 8
i = 9
```

The **while** version, shown in the next example, would produce the same output.

```
/* the while version */

i = 0;                        /* initializer */
while (i<10)          control statement */
{
   printf("i = %d \n",i);
   i++;                       /* incrementor */
}
```

Notice that this loop contains the same three required statements—an initializer, a control statement, and an incrementor. This C-language example, however, shows only a specialized use of the **WHILE** statement; **WHILE** statements are used in many programming languages, and can be used in many other ways.

WHILE and DO Loops

WHILE loops are very much like **IF** statements that can be executed more than once. Every **WHILE** loop has a control statement that, each time the loop is finished running, checks to determine whether the loop should continue to run. (Recall that in the **IF** statement, the control statement only applied the first time through.) The concept behind the **WHILE** loop can be thought of like this:

WHILE *this condition is true*
      Perform these statements
END of WHILE loop

There are several forms of the **WHILE** statement, even within each language. The general forms for each language are discussed in the following sections.

while LOOPS IN C

There are several types of **while** loops in C. The first type is used when there is only a single target statement that needs to be executed during each loop iteration, and when the condition is checked only after the target procedure has been performed at least one time. The general format for this type of loop is:

```
do
      statement;
while (condition);
```

This is saying "Do the following statement while a condition is true." If you need more than one thing to be done in the loop, you would use this format:

```
do
{
   statement1;
   statement2;
}
while (condition);
```

In both of these cases, the target statement(s) in the loop will be executed at least once. Then, if the condition is true, the program will go back to the top of the loop (right after the **do** statement) and execute the target statements again. When the condition becomes false, the program will no longer return to the top of the loop, but instead will continue on to the next statement in the program.

An alternate form of the **while** statement in C evaluates the condition before executing (or disregarding) the loop. If you only need to execute a single target statement, the format for this type of **while** statement looks like this:

```
while (condition)
      statement;
```

For multiple target statements, the format looks like this:

```
while (condition)
{
   statement1;
   statement2;
}
```

In this form of the **while** statement, the condition is evaluated before the loop has a chance to run at all. Therefore, there can be cases where the loop statements are never executed! Here is an example where this would be true:

```
while (10 < 5)
   printf("This should not be printed! \n");
```

Since 10 is never less than 5, the **printf()** statement above would never be executed. However, if you had written this example using the earlier format, it would look like this:

```
do
    printf("This should not be printed! \n");
while (10 < 5);
```

and the statement "This should not be printed!" would be shown on your screen!

The condition in a **while** loop does not have to be a comparison of numbers—it can be as simple as the name of a variable. If the variable has a zero value, it is considered FALSE; otherwise it is TRUE, as shown here:

```
int go;

go=1;
while (go)
{
   printf("The value is now %d \n", go );
   go++;  /* increment go by 1 */
   if (go > 5)
      go = 0;
}
```

In this example, the loop will continue until **go** gets a value greater than 5, which will cause the **if (go > 5)** statement to set the value of **go** to 0. The next time the while statement checks its condition, the loop will stop (since **go** now has a value of 0).

WHILE LOOPS IN PASCAL

There is only one type of **WHILE** loop in Pascal. The condition is always checked before the loop is executed. If you only need to execute a single target statement during each loop iteration, the format for this type of loop is shown here:

```
WHILE condition DO
    statement;
```

If you need to execute multiple statements each time the loop runs successfully, here is the format you should use:

```
WHILE condition DO
BEGIN
    statement1;
    statement2;
END;
```

WHILE LOOPS IN BASIC

There are several types of **WHILE** loops in BASIC. Unlike C and Pascal, BASIC does not require a different format for a single target statement than for multiple statements. In BASIC, as in Pascal, the first type of **WHILE** loop is used when the condition is to be checked before the loop is run (or skipped over). The general format of this type of loop is:

```
WHILE condition
    statements
WEND
```

Notice that the **WHILE** loop in BASIC ends with the **WEND** command (*While END*), and that one or any number of target statements can be placed inside the loop.

An alternate format for this same process is shown here:

```
DO WHILE condition
    statements
LOOP
```

This does not work any differently than the **WHILE..WEND** combination described above. You may want to choose the one you like better and use it consistently. Be sure to check the version of BASIC you are using; some only support either **WHILE..WEND** or **LOOP**, but not both.

Some programmers relate better to the **LOOP** keyword than to **WEND**. There is also a version of the **DO...LOOP** structure that allows for the condition to be checked after the target statements have been run once. The format of this statement is:

DO
      statements
LOOP WHILE *condition*

If you want to make your BASIC code more consistent, you may choose to use the **DO WHILE...LOOP** and **DO...LOOP WHILE** combinations. The **WHILE...WEND** combination may be more confusing.

MORE ABOUT **WHILE** LOOPS

The different **WHILE** loops are nearly identical in purpose. The difference is the timing of execution of the condition statement. With an **IF** statement, the control statement determines whether the line or block of target code would be executed *at all*. With **WHILE** loops, the control statement determines whether the target code will be executed *again*.

note: *In a **WHILE** statement that has the control statement after the target statements, the body of the loop (the target statement or block) will always be executed at least one time. The condition is checked after each execution of the loop. When the control statement is located before the body of the loop, the body of the loop may not be executed at all.*

The next two listings show example programs in C and Pascal, that utilize many of the features you have learned thus far in this chapter.

```
/*
   C Calculator program with loops
*/
#include <stdio.h>

main()
{
    int  go;   /* Boolean variable */
    int  total, one, two;  /* total and two numbers */
    char ch;   /* the command from the user */

    go = 1;  /* true */
```

```
/* OUTER LOOP */

while (go)     /* keep going while this is true */
{
    printf("Enter first number: ");
    scanf(" %d",&one);
    printf("Enter second number: ");
    scanf(" %d",&two);
    printf("Now enter commands to use on these numbers.\n");
    printf("You can use +, -, *, /, or Q to quit, \n");
    printf("or N to enter two different numbers.\n");

    do
    {
        printf(">> ");     /* prompt the user for a command */
        scanf(" %c",&ch); /* this call reads one character
                            from the user, but requires the
                            carriage return to be pressed. */
        switch (ch)
        {
            case '*' : printf(" %d * %d = %d \n", one, two,
                            one*two);
                        break;  /* out of the switch */
            case '/' : if (two == 0)
                            printf("Cannot divide by zero!\n");
                        else
                            printf(" %d / %d = %d \n", one, two,
                                one/two);
                        break;  /* out of the switch */
            case '+' : printf(" %d + %d = %d \n", one, two,
                            one+two);
                        break;  /* out of the switch */
            case '-' : printf(" %d - %d = %d \n", one, two,
                            one-two);
                        break;  /* out of the switch */
            case 'Q' : go = 0;  /* ready to quit now! */
                        break;  /* out of the switch */
        }

        if ((ch == 'Q') || (ch == 'N'))
            break;  /* leave the do loop if user wants to quit
                        or is in need of new numbers */
```

```
    } while (1);  /* end of the do loop */
          /* Remember that in C, 1 , being a non-zero
             value, is the same as True,
             so the above loop continues
             until the break statement is
             executed (when Q or N is pressed. */

    }  /* end of the while loop */
  printf("finished...\n");
}
```

This is a simple calculator program. It asks the user for two numbers (stored in the variables **one** and **two**), and then an operator character. Using the input character, the switch statement determines the correct calculation to perform. The answer is printed, and the user is allowed to enter another operator.

Computer Lingo

Operators are the symbols used in a programming language to denote that some function is being performed. These symbols are not only for use by programmers; mathematicians have traditionally used the + and − operators to represent addition and subtraction. However, because of the difficulties involved in creating characters that look right on computer screens, the symbols commonly used to represent multiplication and division are ★ and /, respectively.

This process continues until the user enters the letter Q or the N. When the Q is typed, the Boolean variable **go** is set to 0 (FALSE). Whether the user enters Q or N, a **break** statement is executed, ending the **do...while** loop. The **while(go)** loop continues as long as the go variable has a non-zero value; it ends when **go** has a zero value (which results when the user enters 0).

In the next example, Pascal is used to perform the same calculator functions:

```
(*
    Pascal Calculator program with loops
*)
program Calc1;

uses CRT;
```

```
VAR
   go : Boolean;
   total, one, two : Integer;
   ch : Char;  { command from the user }

BEGIN {main program}
   go := True;  /* true */

   ( OUTER LOOP *)
```

```
   WHILE go DO    (* keep going while this is true *)
   BEGIN
      Write("Enter first number: ");
      Readln(one);
      Write("Enter second number: ");
      Readln(two);
      Writeln("Now enter commands to use on these numbers.");
      Writeln("You can use +, -, *, /, or Q to quit, or N to ");
      Writeln("enter two different numbers.");

      REPEAT
         Write(">> ");    (* prompt the user for a command *)
         Readln(ch);      (* this call reads one character from
                             the user, but requires the
                             carriage return to be pressed. *)
         CASE ch OF
            '*' : Write(one); Write(" * ");
                  Write(two); Write(" = ");
                  Writeln(one*two);
            '+' : Write(one); Write(" + ");
                  Write(two); Write(" = ");
                  Writeln(one+two);
            '-' : Write(one); Write(" - ");
                  Write(two); Write(" = ");
                  Writeln(one-two);
            '/' : IF two = 0 THEN
                     Writeln("Cannot divide by zero!");
                  ELSE BEGIN
                     Write(one); Write(" / ");
                     Write(two); Write(" = ");
                     Writeln(one/two);
                  END;
            'Q' : go := False; (* ready to quit now! *)
         END;
```

```
    UNTIL (ch = 'Q') OR (ch = 'N');

  END;  (* end of the while loop *)

  Writeln("Finished...");
END {main program}
```

In this example, the outer loop is a **REPEAT...UNTIL** loop. The **RE-PEAT...UNTIL** loop (which will be discussed in the next section) is necessary because Pascal does not support a **WHILE** loop that checks the condition after the target code has been run once. With the exception of this change, the Pascal program works in the same basic manner as the C example.

Computer Lingo

There are times when you will need to use a loop within a block of code that is controlled by another loop. In these cases, the controlling loop is referred to as the *outer loop,* while the loop within is called the *inner loop.*

REPEAT Loops

A **REPEAT** loop (or **REPEAT...UNTIL** loop) can almost be thought of as a backwards **WHILE** loop. In a **WHILE** loop, "WHILE A = TRUE" means that the computer *continues* to execute the target code when A is true, and *stops* the loop when A becomes false, as shown here:

```
WHILE A = TRUE DO
    statement;
END;
```

In a **REPEAT** loop, "UNTIL A = TRUE" means that the computer *continues* to run the loop if A is false, and *stops* the loop when A becomes true, as shown here:

```
REPEAT
    statement;
UNTIL A = TRUE;
```

The only major difference between the **WHILE** and **REPEAT** loops is that in a **REPEAT** loop, the target statement will always be executed at least once (since the condition is not checked until the end of the loop), while in a **WHILE** loop, the statement may never be executed.

REPEAT loops are not available in all languages. Pascal has a **REPEAT** statement, shown here in general form:

```
REPEAT
    statement1;
    statement2;
UNTIL condition;
```

BASIC has a **DO...UNTIL** statement that performs the same function, shown here in general form:

```
DO
    statement1
    statement2
LOOP UNTIL condition
```

The Infamous **GOTO** Statement

There is one last control statement that you should know about. Most languages support a statement called **GOTO**. This is a very powerful—and extremely dangerous—statement. The **GOTO** statement was always popular in early BASIC programming, because one of the only ways to get from one point to another in your program was to **GOTO** a specific line number, as shown in this example:

```
10 PRINT "How old are you?"
20 INPUT Age%
30 IF Age% > 18 GOTO 60
40 PRINT "You are an adult"
50 GOTO 70
60 PRINT "You are not yet an adult"
70 PRINT "See you next time"
```

As you can probably see just from this small example, it can become very difficult to read and trace the execution of this type of program. For this reason, programmers who use the more structured languages (Pascal, Modula-2, C, C++, PL/I, and even the newer versions of BASIC and FORTRAN) have frowned upon the use of the **GOTO** statement. With the variety of looping and control statements now available, **GOTO** can be nearly eliminated. Here is the same program written in Pascal without a **GOTO** statement:

```
(* Pascal program without a GOTO *)
program GotoNot;

uses CRT;

VAR
   Age : Integer;

BEGIN
   Write("How old are you? ");
   Readln(Age);
   IF Age > 18 THEN
      Writeln("You are an adult");
   ELSE
      Writeln("You are not yet an adult");

   Writeln("See you next time");
END
```

If you can avoid using **GOTO** statements, it will save you immense time and effort in the debugging and maintenance of your programs.

Big and Small Pieces

In this chapter, you have learned how to control the flow of a program. In the next chapter, you will learn how programs can be modularized—that is, broken down into smaller pieces. By designing your program as a group of smaller pieces, all working together, you gain several benefits. First of all, you'll be able to find bugs quickly by examining the small part of the program that causes the problems to occur. In addition, you'll be able to save certain pieces of your program individually and reuse them in your future programs.

Chapter 6

What's Coming Up in This Chapter:

An Introduction to Program Design

Creating a Modularized Design

Libraries and APIs

Multifile Projects

Applying What You've Learned

Programming in Pieces

H E tools and techniques that you have learned so far would probably be sufficient for someone who developed only small programs. But even the design of small programs can be improved if you follow certain guidelines. A *software development methodology* is one type of tool that has been created to help make software development more of a science and less of a guessing game. A methodology is simply a set of guidelines that you use for creating your software, starting from the initial design stages.

In this chapter, you will learn a simple software development methodology. You will also discover how programs can be designed in small pieces (called *subroutines, functions,* and *procedures* in various languages), and then put together into one complete program. There are several advantages to this type of programming, which we'll discuss later on.

An Introduction to Program Design

The process of writing a program involves much more than typing in code and watching it run. Programming also involves planning, *modularizing* your program (breaking it into smaller pieces), writing the code, testing, and documentation. Following a good design process allows you to write the program with a minimum number of changes. Not following any design process might mean that the program you write won't do what is expected, and that you'll need to rewrite parts of it.

The following steps are suggested as a strategy for developing any non-trivial program (one that consists of more than a few pages of code). This sequence of steps is based on some of the more common development methodologies now in use. A detailed discussion of these methodologies is beyond the scope of this book; however, the guidelines here should get you started. Figure 6-1 shows a flowchart of these steps.

1. **Determine the purpose of the program.**   Think of all the options that will be required. What will the inputs be? What processing is involved? What outputs will be required?

    For example, a program to calculate loan payments requires input values (length of the loan, amount of the loan, interest rate), processing (calculating the loan payment amount), and output (a printed report showing the input information, the calculations performed on that information, and the final result—a schedule of loan payments).

    This type of design work is often done by a consultant, or a programmer/analyst, who is trying to solve the overall problems that may exist.

2. **Determine program requirements and write them down.**
   If you are designing a small program for your own use, just put this information in a comment at the beginning of the file. If the program is for someone else, or if the program will be larger than a single source file, write this information in a Requirements Document. Your client will either agree that the details of the document are correct, or inform you of areas where the document differs from their needs.

note: *Step 2 may seem like overkill, since you've already determined in Step 1 what the program is to do. However, writing out the established goals of the program, in detail, often helps you work out any problems before it is too late. A written framework lets you show your client (or clarify for yourself) exactly what the program will do, before the code is written. This is the best time to determine any changes necessary in the design, or to find any errors and correct them. In addition, an outline of goals gives you a reference during development, helping you stay focused on what the final program requires.*

3. **Decide what functions should be performed.**   These will usually include input functions, output (or reporting) functions, and functions to perform each of the processing steps. Once the necessary functions have been determined, you can assign and develop separate pieces of the program, called *routines,* to handle each function. This process is called modularizing your program, and it is covered in further detail later in this chapter.

In general, modularizing your program involves determining the main functions that need to be performed, and then breaking each function down into the steps that are required for its completion. If any of these steps seem complicated or unclear, they should be broken down even further. Once you are finished, each of the routines in your program should only be performing a single step of the entire process.

4. **Design the connections between the main program and the separate routines.** A flowchart, pseudocode, or other diagramming technique will help you to create a "roadmap" of the final program. (A sample flowchart and pseudocode will be presented shortly.) You will learn about program routines (also called subroutines, functions, and procedures) later in this chapter.

5. **Write the code, in small modules.** Test each module as it is finished. Each one should relate to a routine that you detailed in Step 3. If the program is large, group related functions in their own separate files; this process will be discussed later in this chapter.

6. **Put the modules together and try the program out as a complete unit.** This is the debugging stage, where you locate and correct any errors in your program. For instance, you may find that the input information does not produce the expected results. You will need to determine the problem: the input may not have been entered correctly, the processing routines may include flawed calculations, or the output routines may be printing the wrong data.

7. **Determine whether the program fulfills the original plan.** If so, pat yourself on the back and go on to Step 8. If not, you need to go back and trace—or repeat—the earlier stages of the development process, as early as Step 3. Your goal here is to find out where changes need to be made to bring the program into agreement with the original plan.

8. **Complete the documentation.** Even if this program is not for anyone but yourself, you need to record how the program was designed so that you can continue to *maintain* it. (As you will recall from Chapter 1, program maintenance involves correcting any bugs that may arise, and making future enhancements.) Your documentation should include all the diagrams and pseudocode that you developed during the programming process, as well as the original discussion of program requirements (from Step 2).

9. **Take a break!**   *Then* start the next project. This break time allows you time to learn from each project, and also helps prevent burnout. Trying to do too much too fast can make even the best programmers less productive.

Figure 6-1

A general sequence of steps for program development

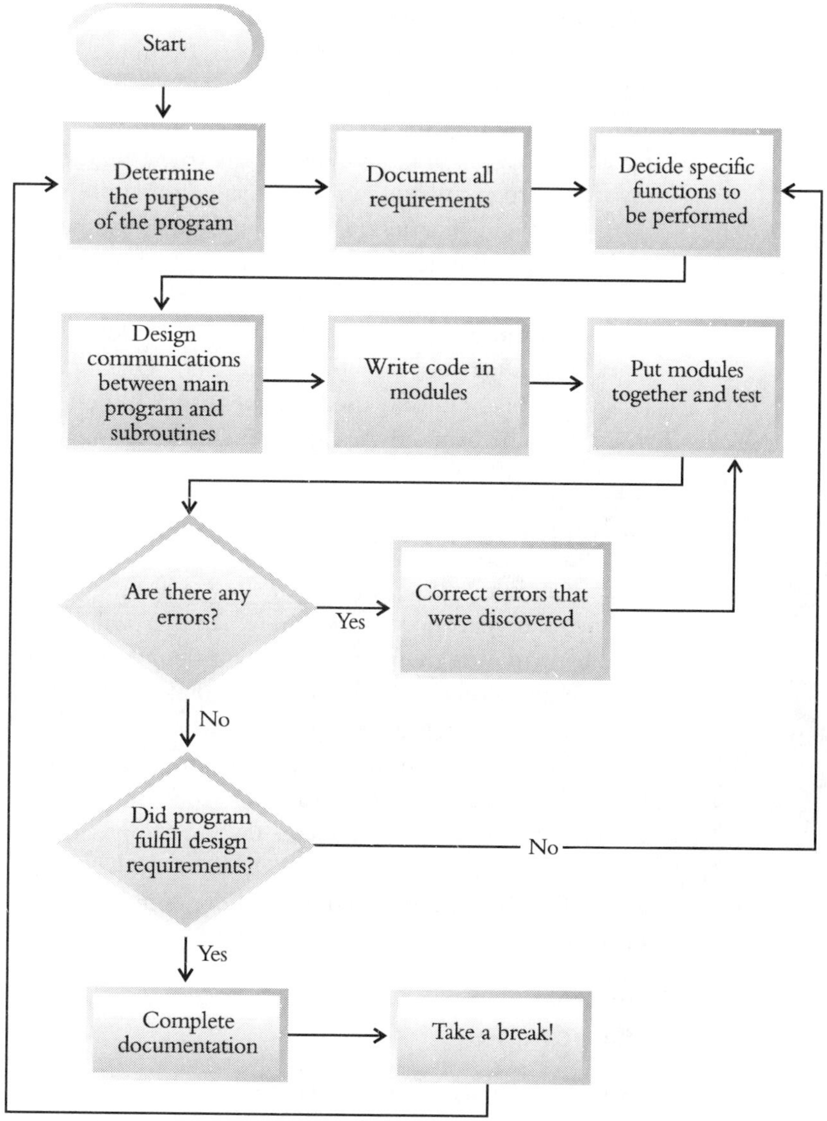

There are many good books available today that cover, often in great detail, how to handle a programming project. (See Appendix D for some of my favorites.) The steps shown above are a combination of several methods, and seem to work well with most projects.

Extremely large projects may require additional planning before the actual code is written, and more exhaustive testing before the program is finished. In these cases, you may want to follow one of the complete software development methodologies used in the programming industry.

Following a formal methodology may seem like just a lot of extra work, but the time invested in producing and documenting a good design is always appreciated during the actual implementation stage. The extra steps imposed by an established methodology often result in less time spent writing and rewriting program code to match changing requirements.

As you begin your design, you should employ some drawing and presentation tools to make the design easier to conceptualize and understand. Each methodology has its own set of drawings to employ, but flow charts and pseudocode are two common tools that programmers use for even the smallest programs. Data Flow Diagrams, Functional Hierarchy Diagrams and Entity Relationship Diagrams are commonly used in larger program design. (These are discussed in more detail below, and in Chapter 8.)

Flowcharts

A *flowchart* is a drawing that shows how a program will operate, the steps that will be followed, and the order in which they will be followed. Flowcharts are used by many programmers as tools for designing programs. Figure 6-2 shows two sample flowcharts. The first example is an overview of the activities necessary for getting up and going to work in the morning, while the second chart shows one part of the process in more detail. While both of these flowcharts include the "Get ready for work" module, they differ in the degree of detail displayed. You may take the same approach with your programming projects: first sketch an overview diagram, to depict the sequence of events at a superficial level, and then prepare more refined diagrams that show the details of each procedure.

Pseudocode

Pseudocode is another popular tool used in program design. *Pseudocode* is a combination of English and the programming language being used, which is

Figure 6-2

Two sample flowcharts: a broad overview, and a more detailed close-up

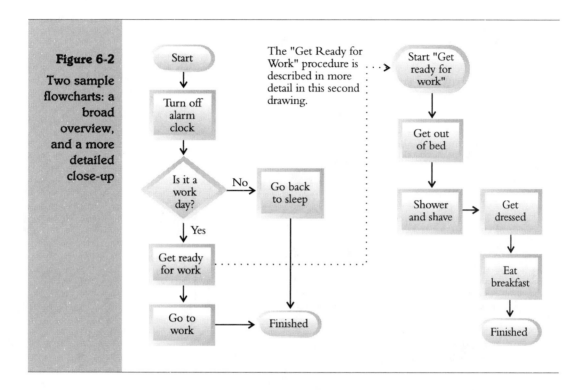

simpler to write and understand than the full source code might be. An example of pseudocode is shown in Figure 6-3, next to the equivalent flowchart. Notice how pseudocode can be simpler to write than flowcharts. This will become more apparent as you start to program on a regular basis.

Other Planning Techniques

Instead of flowcharts, many programmers use a mix of pseudocode and their own types of drawings. The new CASE tools (for *c*omputer-*a*ided *s*oftware *e*ngineering) provide newer diagramming techniques, each specific to one aspect of the design. Some of these diagram types include:

◆ **Data Flow Diagrams (DFDs)** For many programmers, these have replaced flowcharts as the workhorse of program design. A DFD outlines the different functions that need to be performed in a program and, unlike a flowchart, also shows the data that must pass between the functions. The result is a more complete, and often more useful, view of the program. A sample DFD is shown in Figure 6-4.

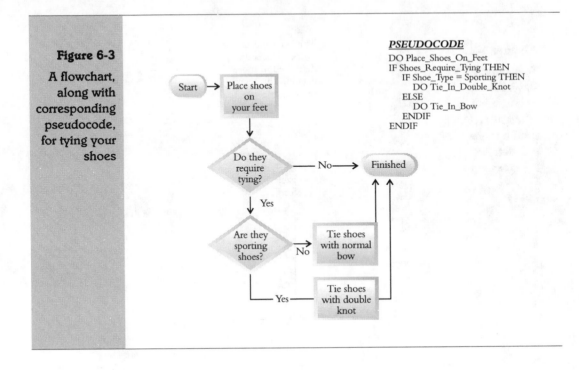

Figure 6-3

A flowchart, along with corresponding pseudocode, for tying your shoes

PSEUDOCODE
```
DO Place_Shoes_On_Feet
IF Shoes_Require_Tying THEN
    IF Shoe_Type = Sporting THEN
        DO Tie_In_Double_Knot
    ELSE
        DO Tie_In_Bow
    ENDIF
ENDIF
```

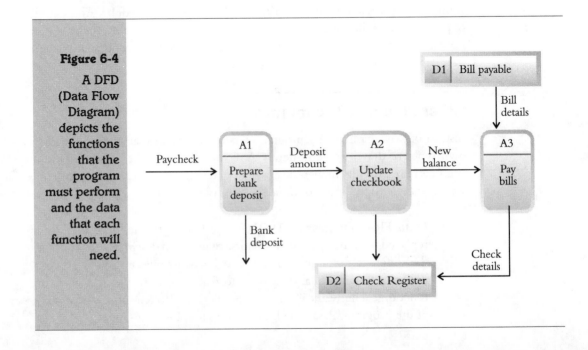

Figure 6-4

A DFD (Data Flow Diagram) depicts the functions that the program must perform and the data that each function will need.

◆ **Function Hierarchy Diagrams (FHDs)** An FHD shows a break-down of the major functions of the program into smaller pieces, and finally to the point where each routine listed can become an actual program module. Unlike DFDs, FHDs do not show any program or data flow; an FHD just shows the major functions in the program, and how they are broken down into smaller subfunctions. A sample FHD is shown in Figure 6-5.

◆ **Entity Relationship Diagrams (ERDs)** An ERD shows what data is being used in the program, how it is stored in files, and how the files are related. ERDs do not show any of the functions of the program, nor the flow of data.

Using a combination of tools can be a very powerful method for software design. Looking at the definitions of DFDs, FHDs, and ERDs above, you can see how their combination could be a powerful development tool. DFDs are best able to display the flow of information into, out of, and throughout your program. FHDs provide a roadmap of the actual functions in your program, and how they are tied together. ERDs are useful in designing the data structures and data files that will be used in your program. CASE tools, and all of these types of drawings, are discussed further in Chapter 8.

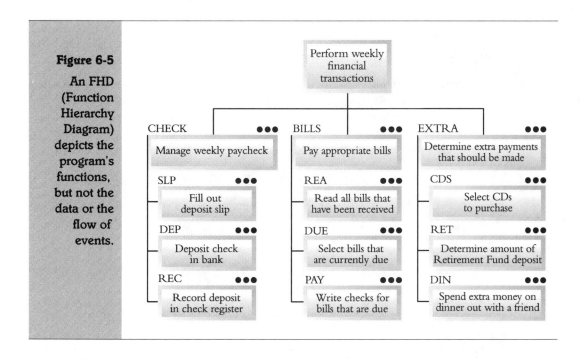

Figure 6-5

An FHD (Function Hierarchy Diagram) depicts the program's functions, but not the data or the flow of events.

Creating a Modularized Design

To make your programs easier to write, debug, and maintain, it is best to break each program into one or more routines. As mentioned earlier, different programming languages refer to routines as functions, procedures, or subroutines.

Computer Lingo	A *function, procedure,* or *subroutine* is a group of program statements that are executed together. This group of statements	has an assigned name, and can be called, invoked, or started from your main program or from within other routines.

Routines are valuable for several reasons. They help break your code into smaller, more understandable pieces. When code is broken into separate routines, other programs (or even other routines within the same program) can reuse the code. Routines allow you to debug a program piece by piece, and localize the problem areas. And finally, by reusing code that works, you can minimize bugs in new programs that you develop.

Program Structure

Before a program is written, you should develop a design for the program, as discussed at the beginning of this chapter. This design should answer the following questions:

- ◆ What should the program do?

- ◆ What input, or data, is required from the user of the program?

- ◆ What processes, or functions, need to be performed on the data?

- ◆ How will the processes that need to be performed be broken down into program routines?

- ◆ What output is expected?

This program design is a road map for writing the program itself.

Once the design is complete, you can begin the coding. For documentation purposes, try to lay out your program files in a consistent manner, breaking each file into several sections. These sections should be separated by comments.

The comments section should contain a discussion of the purpose of the program. If the file does not contain a complete program, the comments should explain the purpose of the functions contained in the current file. Comments vary widely from one programmer to the next, but they should include at least a statement of purpose, the author's name, the date the file was last edited, and the language and compiler that were used. Here is an example of the type of comment you might place at the top of a program file:

```
/*

        Filename:     Parser.C
        Author:       L. John Ribar
                      (Company Name, if relevant)
        Date:         November 1, 1995
        System:       Symantec C++ Professional 6.0

        Purpose:      This file contains code to parse
                      single words out of a sentence,
                      recognizing punctuation and the
                      use of quotations.

    Revision History:

            Date    Who  Changes
            -------- ---  -------------------------------------
            11/01/95 LJR  Original coding
            11/07/95 DJM  Fixed quotation bug
            12/20/95 LJR  Added support for European
                          punctuation changes.
*/
```

Structures and programmer-defined data types used within the file should be described after the comment section, so that another programmer reading the code will immediately know the design of these structures. Here is an example:

```
/********* Structures and Definitions *********/

/* Create a Boolean type */
typedef int Boolean;
```

```
/* Structure for parser tokens */
struct token
{
    char word[80];   /* The word that was parsed */
    char punct;      /* Punctuation or space
                        character that ended the
                        word */
    Boolean more;    /* Is there more left to
                        parse in the sentence? */
};


/****** End Structures and Definitions ******/
```

Next, any global variables should be defined, each with a short comment describing its purpose. Not all languages support the notion of global variables (variables available to all the separate routines); other languages provide *only* global variables. Here is a global definition area:

```
/************* Global Variables *************/

struct token lastToken;   /* last token read */
int tokenCount;           /* number of tokens read */
char sentence[128];       /* sentence being parsed */

/*********** End Global Variables ***********/
```

note: *All variables have a scope in which they are valid. The scope of a variable is that part of the program in which it is valid to use that variable. A variable declared within a routine is only available within that routine, and is often called a* local *variable. A variable declared outside of all routines is available within all of the routines, and is know as a* global *variable. Each language has a method for declaring global variables.*

If you develop the habit of laying out your files in a consistent manner, it will be much simpler to locate the various pieces of a program when you are in a hurry, under a deadline, or searching diligently for a defect. In addition, when you come back at a later date to make changes to a program, the layout will serve as a table of contents, helping you locate various parts of the program.

Functions, Procedures and Subroutines

Each program routine should be designed with a single purpose in mind. Perhaps the routine has inputs and outputs. Perhaps it is not designed to have any interaction with a larger, main program. In any case, the routine must have a clear purpose, which should be determined in advance and then followed as the code is written. It is good programming practice to place a comment at the beginning of every routine to detail its purpose and to list any expected inputs, as well as the desired outputs.

In some languages (such as FORTRAN and BASIC), you use a **CALL** statement to invoke, or start, a function. In C and Pascal, just using the function's name in your program, followed by parentheses, invokes the function. The values or variables that are *passed* (sent) into the function are called *parameters*. The parameters are placed between the parentheses when the function is called, as shown in this Pascal example:

```
Write("This is a test. My age is ");
Writeln(32);
```

Here, two procedure calls are made. The first call, to the procedure **Write()**, has a character string parameter, namely "This is a test. My age is ". The second call, to the procedure **Writeln()**, has an integer parameter of 32.

In the following C example, three parameters are passed to the **printf()** function.

```
printf("My name is %s, and I am %d years old \n",
       "John", 32 );
```

The parameters are two strings ("My name is %s, and I am %d years old \n" and "John") and an integer (32).

There is a good deal of similarity between C, Pascal, and BASIC in dealing with functions, parameter passing, and return values. However, there are also a few major differences. The following three programs show some of these similarities and differences.

```
/*
    Program:     C Demo of functions
    Author:      L. John Ribar, Programming Primer
    Date:        October 15, 1995
*/
```

```c
#include <stdio.h>   /* allow for screen writes */

/* First define the routines. These are known
   in C as Prototypes */
int DoubleIt( int i );
void SquareIt( int *i );

/* Main program */

main()   /* main C routine */
{
    int aNumber, sNumber;

    aNumber = DoubleIt( 5 );
    printf("5 doubled is %d \n", aNumber);
    sNumber = aNumber;
    SquareIt( &sNumber );
    printf("%d doubled is %d \n", aNumber, sNumber);

}


/*
   Function which returns an integer value,
   which is twice the number passed in.
*/
int DoubleIt( int i )
{
    return i*2;
}

/*
   Function which squares the number passed in,
   and returns it in the same variable.
*/
void SquareIt( int *i )
{
    *i = (*i) * (*i);
        /* The parentheses around *i are not
           necessary; they make reading the
           multiplication statement simpler! */
}
```

In C, all of the routines that you write are called functions; the words *subroutine* and *procedure* are not used at all.

In C and C++, you must create prototypes for your functions. A *prototype* is a statement that shows how the function is called, what parameters are expected, what type of data each parameter will be, and the data type of the return value. In fact, it should look just like the first line of the actual function. There are two prototypes at the beginning of the above program, one for **DoubleIt()** and one for **SquareIt()**.

The prototype for **DoubleIt()** shows that it takes one parameter (an integer named **i**), and returns an integer value. **SquareIt()**, on the other hand, takes a parameter that is a pointer to an integer (denoted with the ***** before the variable name), and has no return value. This is shown with the **void** keyword.

remember: *Pointers are variables that point to specific memory locations. In C, they are used to pass these memory locations between functions, allowing data to be changed within each function.*

Notice that when each of these functions is written later in the program, the prototype becomes the first line of the function. This insures that the right types of variables are passed into the functions. If you try to call one of these functions with the wrong type of data, the compiler will display an error message or a warning.

In the next example, you will see how these same routines are programmed in Pascal.

```
PROGRAM PROCFUNC;
(*
    Program:  Pascal Demo of Functions and Procedures
    Author:   L. John Ribar, Programming Primer
    Date:     October 15, 1995
*)

Uses CRT;  (* allow printing to screen *)

(* Global Variables *)
VAR
    sNumber,
    aNumber : Integer;

(*
    Function that returns a number twice the
    number passed in.
*)
```

```pascal
FUNCTION DoubleIt( i : Integer ) : Integer;
BEGIN
   DoubleIt := i * 2;
END;

(*
   Procedures which squares the number passed in,
   and returns it in the same variable.
*)
PROCEDURE SquareIt( VAR i : Integer );
BEGIN
   i := i * i;
END;

BEGIN {main program}
   aNumber := DoubleIt( 5 );
   WriteLn("5 doubled is ", aNumber);
   sNumber := aNumber;
   SquareIt( sNumber );
   WriteLn(aNumber," squared is ",sNumber);
END
```

Notice that, unlike C, Pascal has one name (**FUNCTION**) for routines that return values, and another name (**PROCEDURE**) for those that do not. Also, Pascal places the keyword **VAR** in front of any parameter that will be changed in the function or procedure. Using **VAR** with a parameter actually causes Pascal to pass a pointer, like C, but this happens without any work on the part of the programmer. Thus Pascal programmers do not have to use pointer variables as often within their functions and procedures, as do C programmers.

You may also notice that Pascal does not make you predefine the subroutines and functions, as C and BASIC do. However, this means that your routines must be placed in the file in the correct order: You must define each function or subroutine (using the equivalent of a prototype) before it is called from the main program or from another routine.

In the next example, you will see how BASIC handles subroutines and functions.

```basic
' Program:   BASIC Functions and SUBroutines
' Author:    L. John Ribar, Programming Primer
' Date:      October 15, 1995
```

```
' First, define the routines. This is similar
' to C Prototypes
DECLARE SUB SquareIt (num AS INTEGER)
DECLARE FUNCTION DoubleIt! (num AS INTEGER)

' Main Program
aNumber% = DoubleIt(5)
PRINT "5 doubled is ", aNumber%
sNumber% = aNumber%
CALL SquareIt(sNumber%)
PRINT aNumber%, " squared is ", sNumber%
END

' Function that returns a number twice the number
' passed in.
FUNCTION DoubleIt! (num AS INTEGER)
   DoubleIt = num * 2
END FUNCTION

' Procedures which squares the number
' passed in, and returns it in the same variable.
SUB SquareIt (num AS INTEGER)
   num = num * num
END SUB
```

Like C, many BASIC compilers force you to predefine the functions and subroutines that you will be writing, so that the compiler can check for the correct data types in your calls to these routines.

To define a data type for the return value in BASIC, you simply use the special character reserved for that data type. For instance, in the example above, the function **DoubleIt!** will return a single precision real number (denoted by the ! character).

In QBASIC, enclosing the parameters in parentheses will prevent them from being changed in the function or subroutine. Therefore, the following BASIC calling sequence

```
SquareIt sNumber%
```

would allow **sNumber%** to be changed within the subroutine, while

```
SquareIt(sNumber%)
```

would not allow the **SquareIt** subroutine to change the value of **sNumber%**.

Most of the newest BASIC compilers and interpreters allow subroutines and functions, as shown in the preceding example. Older BASIC compilers did not use these methods of defining and calling procedures; if you look at older BASIC code, you will see the use of **GOSUB** statements.

A **GOSUB** (*GO* to *SUB*routine) call is used to jump from one location in the program to another, and then to return to the original location once the necessary processing is finished at the new location. The **GOSUB** call works much like a subroutine, but it cannot have any parameters or return values! An example is shown here:

```
10 REM BASIC example of GOSUB calls
20 REM Author:   L. John Ribar, Programming Primer
30 REM Date:     October 15, 1995
40 FOR i% = 1 TO 10
50    GOSUB 100
60 NEXT i%
70 END
100 REM "Subroutine"
110 PRINT i%, i% * i%, i% * i% * i%
120 RETURN
```

Since no parameters or return values are allowed, the main program must load a global variable (**i%** in this case) with a value, and then **GOSUB** line 100. In the "subroutine," the global data is used to print the value of **i%**, along with its square and cube values.

Libraries and APIs

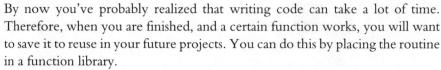

By now you've probably realized that writing code can take a lot of time. Therefore, when you are finished, and a certain function works, you will want to save it to reuse in your future projects. You can do this by placing the routine in a function library.

A *function library* is a special file that contains whatever routines you have placed there. It is accessed by the compiler when you build a program, so that all the routines you have stored from previous projects are available to your current programs.

Of course, you are not the only programmer around. Other programmers have also written excellent pieces of code, and have placed them in libraries of their own. When you look through programming magazines, some of the advertisements you see are for this type of library. Libraries are available for graphic functions, mathematics, user interfaces, serial communications, and much more.

Once you have one or more of these libraries, you can use the procedures in them just as if they were built into your programming language. For instance, if you are accustomed to using a statement like this one to display a name on the screen,

```
printf("Hello, %s\n", name)
```

you may get a library that prints to a window, or in a special font, and then be able to call it in a similar fashion, perhaps like this:

```
wprintf( window, "Hello, %s \n", name);
```

Some libraries are referred to as *APIs*, or *Application Programming Interfaces*. These are usually used for special purposes. For instance, there is an API designed specifically for the Microsoft Windows operating environment. The API is simply a published set of function calls that can be made to support a particular environment; the Windows API includes functions that allow you to write programs for the Windows environment. The API is simply the list of procedure or function names that can be called by your program. APIs are generally used to create programming standards that can be used across operating environment and compiler boundaries.

Multifile Projects

One thing you haven't yet seen in this book is a program that uses multiple source code files. Think about it, however; when you have created functions that you want to reuse, they will probably reside in multiple files, scattered all over your disk.

For this reason, there are special tools, called Make utilities, created especially to make multifile programming simpler. A *Make utility* uses a special file, which you create, called a makefile. The *makefile* has commands in it that indicate which source files your program should use, and which files are dependent on others. By using a Make utility to keep track of your source code, you can ensure that only the minimal number of files will be recompiled when you make changes to your program.

Here is an example of a makefile for a larger project:

```
# Makefile for Picasso CraneSim Environment

#-------------------------------------------------
# Definitions
#-------------------------------------------------

MODEL = 1
BLINK = D:\BCPP\B2
CC = bcc
flags = -m$(MODEL) -Vs
myobjs = cranesim.obj gadgets.obj craneset.obj \
         genset.obj satset.obj runsim.obj \
         tinplong.obj tcolortx.obj menus.obj \
         hint.obj about.obj

#-------------------------------------------------
# Dependencies
#-------------------------------------------------

cranesim.exe : $(myobjs) makefile cranesim.lnk
               $(BLINK)\blinker @cranesim.lnk

cranesim.obj : cranesim.cpp cranesim.h gadgets.h \
               setup.h

menus.obj : menus.cpp cranesim.h gadgets.h hint.h

gadgets.obj : gadgets.cpp gadgets.h

craneset.obj : cranesim.cpp setup.h

genset.obj : genset.cpp setup.h

satset.obj : satset.cpp setup.h

runsim.obj : runsim.cpp setup.h

tcolortx.obj : tcolortx.h

hint.obj : hint.cpp hint.h

about.obj : about.cpp setup.h
```

```
#──────────────────────────────── -
# Rules
#──────────────────────────────── -

.cpp.obj:
    $(CC) -c $(flags) {$< }
```

As you can see, a makefile can include several types of commands. In the Definitions area, several macros are defined. Macros are replaced by the Make program any time they occur in the file. For instance, the listing above contains the following lines:

```
MODEL = 1
BLINK = D:\BCPP\B2
CC = bcc
flags = -m$(MODEL) -Vs
```

Each of these lines is a macro. Every time the word **$(MODEL)** appears in the makefile, the letter l will be inserted. Likewise, any place the word **$(flags)** appears, the string **-ml -Vs** will be inserted. (Notice that the **MODEL** macro was replaced first!) Therefore, this line

```
$(CC) -c $(flags) {$< }
```

will be replaced with the following line, sent to the compiler, when the macros **CC** and **flags** are replaced. This replacement occurs when the Make program itself is run, using the makefile as input. The replacement will be

```
bcc -c -ml -Vs filename.c
```

where **filename.c** is the name of the file that is being compiled.

In the Dependencies area, you can see a list of relationships between files. The name of each dependent file is followed by a colon and one or more other filenames that the first file is dependent upon. For example, this line

```
menus.obj : menus.cpp cranesim.h gadgets.h hint.h
```

says that the **menus.obj** file depends on the files **menu.cpp**, **cranesim.h**, **gadgets.h**, and **hint.h**. Therefore, if any of those four files change, the **menus.obj** file needs to be recompiled.

There are a great number of features available in the newest Make utilities, and this discussion has probably only whet your appetite to learn more. Luckily, almost every good compiler now comes with a Make utility—allowing programmers to focus more on programming, and less on file tracking!

Applying What You've Learned

So far, you have seen a lot of sample code and a few small programs. You've also learned about the software development process. Now you are ready to try an entire project on your own. You may not have a computer handy, but that is not a problem. In the next chapter, you will be given a program to write. If you can apply what you have learned, you will be doing fine, even without a computer.

After all, for many years, programming courses did not use computers at all! Early computers were simply too big and expensive to be used by just anyone—especially programmers in training. Also, before the PC revolution put a computer on every desktop, there were fewer computers around, and access to them was generally reserved for experienced programmers with actual work to be done. An even more serious obstacle to neophyte programmers was that early computers were much more susceptible to failure than today's models are; any wrong move could cause a crash. Why inflict that kind of stress on a freshman?

So if you don't have a computer to use, go ahead and program on paper for now. Once you've mastered the concepts, you'll have plenty of time to pick a compiler and start doing the real thing.

Chapter 7

Pulling It All Together

A manager went to the master programmer and showed him the requirements document for a new application. The manager asked the master: "How long will it take to design this system if I assign five programmers to it?"

"It will take one year," said the master promptly.

"But we need this system immediately or even sooner! How long will it take if I assign ten programmers to it?"

The master programmer frowned. "In that case, it will take two years."

"And what if I assign a hundred programmers to it?"

The master programmer shrugged. "Then the design will never be completed," he said.

—The Tao of Programming

I F you have read up to this point in the book, you have learned a good deal about programming fundamentals. But the best way to really learn programming is through doing it, getting your hands dirty, trying it out on your own. This chapter gives you an actual programming assignment; you'll have the opportunity to develop an entire application, using the techniques and language elements you have been learning all along. Before you look at the solutions, be sure to try things on your own—this is the very best way to learn programming!

What Your Program Must Do

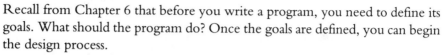

Recall from Chapter 6 that before you write a program, you need to define its goals. What should the program do? Once the goals are defined, you can begin the design process.

Here are the requirements for the program to be created in this chapter: Your program will read a number and the name of a payee from the user. Then, a check will be generated. The payee and amount will be printed on the check, along with the spelled-out version of the amount. For instance, if the program prompts the user and receives the following entries,

```
Who is the payee: Smith Brothers
Enter your number: 155.10
```

then it should respond with

```
Pay to the Order of Smith Brothers ........$155.10

One hundred Fifty Five dollars and Ten cents
```

For this program, you will need to be concerned with the following issues:

◆ Data entry from the user—both numeric and string input

◆ Subroutines and their functions

◆ Output to the screen

◆ Mathematical functions to determine which numeric words need to be printed

◆ Manipulation of text strings for printing numeric values as words

Now that you have the requirements, try to design the functions that need to be performed; then, move on to the next section to see one design solution.

The Program's Design

What functions will you define for the program? Each of the functions you specify should become the basis for a module, or subroutine. In that way, your

program will look similar in structure to the original design, and it will be simpler to test the final results against the original requirements.

The major functions that should be performed are:

◆ Reading data from the user

◆ Printing the payee's name and the amount on the top line of the check

◆ Determining the number of dollars and the number of cents

◆ Printing the number of dollars in words

◆ Printing the words "dollars and"

◆ Printing the number of cents in words

◆ Printing the word "cents"

A simple flowchart displaying these steps is shown in Figure 7–1.

Most of the functions required for this program are rather straightforward. Two of them, however, might benefit from additional discussion. First, how do you determine the numbers of dollars and cents that need to be printed? Here is one simple method:

1. Assign **NUM** to an integer variable called **DOLLARS**.

2. Subtract **DOLLARS** from **NUM**. This will leave only the cents portion of **NUM**, with the number of dollars safe in **DOLLARS**.

3. Multiply **NUM** by 100. This will make the cents into a number between 0 and 100.

4. Assign **NUM** to an integer variable called **CENTS**. You now have the two parts of the number stored in **DOLLARS** and **CENTS**.

Second, how do you convert a number into words? Here is a brief overview of the process. As you read through these steps, try them out on a piece of paper with the number 155, just to see what is happening. Then compare what you've written to the sample pseudocode that follows each step.

Tip: *This section assumes that the number is less than 1000. Adding the capability for higher numbers will be a good exercise for you later on!*

Figure 7-1

A flowchart for the assigned program

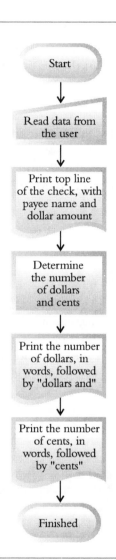

1. Determine the number of hundreds available by dividing your variable **NUM** (155) by 100. Make sure the result is stored in an integer variable. If the result is greater than one, print the appropriate number, and the word "hundred".

```
155 / 100 = 1.55

1.55 equals 1 as an integer, so
Print "one" and then "hundred".
```

2. Subtract the hundreds from **NUM**. This is done by multiplying the integer returned in Step 1 by 100, and then subtracting the result from **NUM**. In this example, **NUM** will now equal 55.

```
155 - (1 * 100) = 55
```

3. Now divide **NUM** by 10 to determine the number of tens. Again, be sure to store the result in an integer variable. If the result is greater than or equal to 2, print the appropriate number and, again, subtract the tens from **NUM**. In this example, **NUM** will now equal 5.

```
55 / 10 = 5
Print "fifty"
55 - (5 * 10) = 5
```

4. Print the number that is left, 5 in this case.

This process changes slightly when the number of tens returned in Step 3 is 1 (that is, when the rightmost two digits of the check amount are between 9 and 20). If this is the case, you need to print the teen value (*fifteen* rather than *ten-ty 5*, for example). This will be covered in the example programs below.

The Solutions

The three programs that follow are all possible answers for the check-writing program. Each is somewhat different, showing how each respective language might deal with the requirements of the program.

Pascal

Here is a Pascal solution to the project. Read through the comments in this program for a better understanding of Pascal-specific programming issues.

```
(* Program to print out a check, with words        *)

(* Author:    L. John Ribar, Programming Primer   *)
(* Date:      18 October 1995                      *)
(* System:    Borland Turbo Pascal                 *)
```

```
Program DoCheck;

Uses CRT;  (* allows input and output *)
(* Subroutines come first in a Pascal program *)

Procedure PrintNum( i : Integer )
CONST
    (* for this function, declare a set of strings,
       with the names we need. This uses the Turbo
       Pascal 'typed constant' capability. The
       NumberNames array can in this way be set
       with all the correct values. *)
    NumberNames : ARRAY [1..9] OF STRING =
         ("One ", "Two ", "Three ", "Four ", "Five ",
         "Six ", "Seven ", "Eight ", "Nine ");
BEGIN
    (* Now, select a string based on the value passed
       into the function. *)
    Write(NumberNames[i]);
END;  (* PrintNum *)

Procedure PrintTeen( t : Integer )
BEGIN
    (* For this function, use a CASE statement. This
       is done because the values of t are not starting
       at 1, so there would be a lot of empty strings
       if an array was used. *)
    CASE t OF
       10 : Write("Ten ");
       11 : Write("Eleven ");
       12 : Write("Twelve ");
       13 : Write("Thirteen ");
       14 : Write("Fourteen ");
       15 : Write("Fifteen ");
       16 : Write("Sixteen ");
       17 : Write("Seventeen ");
       18 : Write("Eighteen ");
       19 : Write("Nineteen ");
    END;  (* case *)
END;  (* PrintTeen *)

Procedure PrintTen( t : Integer )
BEGIN
    (* For this function, use a CASE statement. An
```

```
                      array could also have been used. *)
          CASE t OF
             2 : Write("Twenty ");
             3 : Write("Thirty ");
             4 : Write("Forty ");
             5 : Write("Fifty ");
             6 : Write("Sixty ");
             7 : Write("Seventy ");
             8 : Write("Eighty ");
             9 : Write("Ninety ");
          END;  (* case *)
       END;  (* PrintTen *)


       Procedure PrintWords( num : Integer )
       VAR
          (* Declare some local variables *)
          Hund, Tens : Integer;
       BEGIN
          (* First, how many hundreds? *)
          Hund := num / 100.0;
          IF Hund > 0 THEN
          BEGIN
             PrintNum (Hund);
             Write("hundred ");
             (* Subtract the hundreds *)
             num := num - (Hund * 100);
          END;  (* if *)


          (* Now determine number of tens *)
          Tens := num / 10.0;
          CASE Tens OF
             0 : ;  (* ignore zero! *)
             1 :
                PrintTeen( Integer(num) );
                (* If a teen number was printed, no
                   more work is required. *)
                num := 0;
             ELSE (* for all the rest (2-9) *)
             BEGIN
                PrintTen( Tens );
                num := num - (Tens * 10);
             END;
          END;  (* case *)
```

```
    (* Print the final number *)
    IF num > 0 THEN PrintNum( Integer(num) );
}

(* Declare the variables needed in main program *)
VAR
    Payee : ARRAY [1..40] OF CHAR;
    AmtDue : REAL;
    Dollars, Cents : Integer;

BEGIN (* start main program *)

    (* First get the data from the user *)
    Write("Who is the Payee: ");
    ReadLn( Payee );
    Write("How much is owed: ");
    ReadLn( AmtDue );
    WriteLn(); (* skip a line *)

    (* Print the first line of the check *)
    Write("Pay to the order of ", Payee );
    WriteLn(".............", AmtDue );

    (* Determine dollars and cents *)
    Dollars := AmtDue;
    Cents := (AmtDue - Dollars) * 100.0;

    (* Now print the words *)
    IF Dollars = 0 THEN
        Write("No dollars and ");
    ELSE
    BEGIN
        PrintWords (Dollars);
        Write("dollars and ");
    END; (* if *)

    IF Cents = 0 THEN
        WriteLn("No cents");
    ELSE
    BEGIN
        PrintWords (Cents);
        WriteLn("cents");
    END; (* if *)

END  (* end of main program *)
```

The Pascal solution is broken up into several routines, which are discussed next.

PROCEDURE PrintNum()

This procedure receives an integer and then prints the text name of that integer. In the Pascal solution, an array of words is used. The array is called **NumberNames**, and there are nine entries in it, one for each of the digits. You will notice that the word in a position matches the number of that position; for instance, **NumberNames[1]** (the first element in the array) is "One".

PROCEDURE PrintTeen()

This procedure receives an integer, assumed to be a number from 10 to 19; any other number will be ignored. In **PrintTeen()**, a **CASE** statement is used to print the verbal representation of the number passed in.

This could also be done with an array, but an additional calculation on the number would have to be made. For instance, if you store the numbers in array elements 1 through 10, then in order to print the correct word you would need to subtract 9 from each number passed in.

PROCEDURE PrintTen()

This procedure prints the correct multiple of 10, based on the parameter passed. This could be done with an array, but you would need to number the array from 2 through 9.

PROCEDURE PrintWords()

The **PrintWords()** procedure performs most of the work in this program. It determines the number of hundreds, tens, and ones, according to algorithms discussed earlier in this chapter. It also determines if the tens and ones make a teen number.

Using the numbers calculated, the appropriate **PrintNum()**, **PrintTen()**, and **PrintTeen()** procedures are called.

THE MAIN PROGRAM

The main part of this program is rather simple. The name of the payee and the amount of the check are read from the user. The top part of the check is printed, and then the number of dollars and the number of cents are calculated, using the algorithms described earlier. Finally, **PrintWords()** is called for both the dollar amount and the cent amount.

BASIC

Here is a BASIC solution to the project. Read through the comments in this program for a better understanding of BASIC-specific programming issues.

```
' Program to print out a check, with words
' Author:       L. John Ribar, Programming Primer
' Date:         18 October 1995
' System:       Microsoft QBASIC

' Declare all the subroutines
DECLARE SUB PrintTen (t AS INTEGER)
DECLARE SUB PrintTeen (t AS INTEGER)
DECLARE SUB PrintWords (NUM AS INTEGER)
DECLARE SUB PrintNum (i AS INTEGER)

' First get the data from the user
PRINT "Who is the Payee: ";
INPUT Payee$
PRINT "How much is owed: ";
INPUT AmtDue#

' Print the first line of the check
PRINT "Pay to the order of "; Payee$;
PRINT USING "&    $$,,,,.##"; "............"; AmtDue#

' Determine dollars and cents
Dollars% = INT(AmtDue#)
Cents% = (AmtDue# - Dollars%) * 100

' Now print the words
IF Dollars% = 0 THEN
   PRINT "No dollars and ";
ELSE
   PrintWords (Dollars%)
   PRINT "dollars and ";
END IF

IF Cents% = 0 THEN
   PRINT "No cents"
```

```
        ELSE
           PrintWords (Cents%)
           PRINT "cents"
        END IF

        END

        SUB PrintNum (i AS INTEGER)
           SELECT CASE i
              CASE 1
                 PRINT "One ";
              CASE 2
                 PRINT "Two ";
              CASE 3
                 PRINT "Three ";
              CASE 4
                 PRINT "Four ";
              CASE 5
                 PRINT "Five ";
              CASE 6
                 PRINT "Six ";
              CASE 7
                 PRINT "Seven ";
              CASE 8
                 PRINT "Eight ";
              CASE 9
                 PRINT "Nine ";
           END SELECT
        END SUB

        SUB PrintTeen (t AS INTEGER)
           SELECT CASE t
              CASE 10
                 PRINT "Ten ";
              CASE 11
                 PRINT "Eleven ";
              CASE 12
                 PRINT "Twelve ";
              CASE 13
                 PRINT "Thirteen ";
              CASE 14
                 PRINT "Fourteen ";
              CASE 15
                 PRINT "Fifteen ";
```

```
      CASE 16
         PRINT "Sixteen ";
      CASE 17
         PRINT "Seventeen ";
      CASE 18
         PRINT "Eighteen ";
      CASE 19
         PRINT "Nineteen ";
   END SELECT

END SUB

SUB PrintTen (t AS INTEGER)
   SELECT CASE t
      CASE 2
         PRINT "Twenty ";
      CASE 3
         PRINT "Thirty ";
      CASE 4
         PRINT "Forty ";
      CASE 5
         PRINT "Fifty ";
      CASE 6
         PRINT "Sixty ";
      CASE 7
         PRINT "Seventy ";
      CASE 8
         PRINT "Eighty ";
      CASE 9
         PRINT "Ninety ";
   END SELECT

END SUB

SUB PrintWords (NUM AS INTEGER)
   ' First, how many hundreds? Round it down using
   ' the INT() function
   Hund% = INT(NUM / 100)
   IF Hund% > 0 THEN
      PrintNum (Hund%)
      PRINT "hundred ";
      ' Subtract the hundreds
      NUM = NUM - (Hund% * 100)
   END IF
```

```
' Now determine number of tens
Tens% = INT(NUM / 10)
SELECT CASE Tens%
    CASE 2 TO 9
        PrintTen (Tens%)
        NUM = NUM - (Tens% * 10)
    CASE 1
        PrintTeen (INT(NUM))
        ' If we printed a teen number, no more
        ' work is required.
        NUM = 0
END SELECT

' Print the final number
IF NUM > 0 THEN PrintNum (NUM)

END SUB
```

The BASIC solution is also broken up into several routines, which are discussed next.

THE MAIN PROGRAM

The first part of this program that is different from the Pascal solution is the definition of the subroutines at the top of the program. This is done so that the compiler can check the procedures and parameters as they are called throughout the program. This is not required in Pascal, because the procedures are defined before they are used.

The main part of this program is rather simple. The name of the payee and the amount of the check are read from the user. The top part of the check is printed, and then the number of dollars and the number of cents are calculated, using the algorithms discussed earlier in this chapter. Finally, **PrintWords()** is called for both the dollars and cents amounts.

The printing of the check amount uses the **PRINT USING** command. This command is similar in concept to the **printf()** function in C; it allows numbers to be printed with specific formatting. In this case, the formatting is

```
"&    $$,,,,.##"
```

The **&** symbol is used to print out the string value ("............"). The **$$** causes the number that is output to start with a dollar sign. The series of commas mean that commas should be inserted every three characters. After the period are two **#** symbols. These instruct the **PRINT** statement to always print two decimal places.

SUBROUTINE PrintNum

This subroutine receives an integer and then prints the text name of that integer. In the Pascal solution, an array of words was used. Since there is not a simple, standard method for defining the values of an array in BASIC, a **SELECT CASE** statement is used here instead. Each **CASE** is for a specific digit (one through nine); once the correct number is determined, the appropriate word is printed.

SUBROUTINE PrintTeen

This subroutine receives an integer, assumed to be a number from 10 to 19; any other number will be ignored. As in **PrintNum**, a **SELECT CASE** statement is used to print the verbal representation of the number passed in.

SUBROUTINE PrintTen

This subroutine prints the correct multiple of 10, based on the parameter passed. It is nearly identical to **PrintNum** and **PrintTeen**, but prints a different set of names.

SUBROUTINE PrintWords

The **PrintWords** subroutine procedure performs most of the work in this program. It determines the number of hundreds, tens, and ones, according to the algorithms described earlier. It also determines if the tens and ones make a teen number.

Using the numbers calculated, the correct combination of **PrintNum**, **PrintTen**, and **PrintTeen** are called.

C Language

Here is a C-language solution to the project. Read through the comments in this program for a better understanding of C-specific programming issues.

```
/* Program to print out a check, with words    */
/* Author:      L. John Ribar, Programming Primer */
```

```
/* Date:        18 October 1995                    */
/* System:      Borland C/C++                      */

#include <stdio.h>  /* allows input and output */
#include <string.h> /* allows use of strlen() */

/* Prototypes for all the functions */
void PrintTen( int t );
void PrintTeen( int t );
void PrintWords( int num );
void PrintNum( int i );

void main() /* start main program */
{
   /* Declare the variables needed */
   char Payee[40];
   float AmtDue;
   int Dollars, Cents;
   int p;

   /* First get the data from the user */
   printf("Who is the Payee: ");
   fgets( Payee, 40, stdin );
   /* The fgets() function includes the carriage
      return in the string. So before going on,
      remove the carriage return. It is the last
      thing in the string. */
   /* First determine the length of the string */
   p = strlen(Payee);
   /* Now put a zero in the last position, where
      the carriage return currently sits. */
   Payee[p-1] = 0;

   printf("How much is owed: ");
   scanf(" %f", &AmtDue );
   printf("\n"); /* skip a line */

   /* Print the first line of the check */
   printf("Pay to the order of %s", Payee );
   printf(" %s   $%9.2f \n", "............", AmtDue );

   /* Determine dollars and cents */
   /* Here, you need to use the C "cast" function, to
      make variables of one type look like another type.
```

```
        Thus, (int) makes the float look like an integer
        and (float) makes the integer look like a
        floating point number. */
   Dollars = (int) AmtDue;
   Cents = (int) ((AmtDue - (float) Dollars) * 100.0);

   /* Now print the words */
   if ( Dollars == 0 )
      printf("No dollars and ");
   else
   {
      PrintWords (Dollars);
      printf("dollars and ");
   }

   if ( Cents == 0 )
      printf("No cents \n");
   else
   {
      PrintWords (Cents);
      printf("cents \n");
   }

}  /* end of main program */

void PrintNum( int i )
{
   /* for this function, declare a set of strings,
      with the names we need. */
   char *NumberNames[9] =
      {
         "One ", "Two ", "Three ", "Four ", "Five ",
         "Six ", "Seven ", "Eight ", "Nine "
      };

   /* Now, select a string based on the value passed
      into the function. Remember: you must subtract
      one to get the right array element. */
   printf(NumberNames[i-1]);
}


void PrintTeen( int t )
{
   /* For this function, use a switch statement. This
```

```
             is done because the values of t are not starting
             at 1, so there would be a lot of empty strings
             if an array was used. */
      switch (t)
      {
          case 10 : printf("Ten "); break;
                    /* Remember, the break statement is
                       necessary so that the program won't
                       drop down into the next case. */
          case 11 : printf("Eleven "); break;
          case 12 : printf("Twelve "); break;
          case 13 : printf("Thirteen "); break;
          case 14 : printf("Fourteen "); break;
          case 15 : printf("Fifteen "); break;
          case 16 : printf("Sixteen "); break;
          case 17 : printf("Seventeen "); break;
          case 18 : printf("Eighteen "); break;
          case 19 : printf("Nineteen "); break;
      }
}


void PrintTen( int t )
{
   /* For this function, use a switch statement. This
      is done because the values of t are not contiguous,
      that is, they jump by ten each time. This would
      cause a great number of empty strings if an
      array was used. */
   switch (t)
   {
       case 2 : printf("Twenty "); break;
                /* Remember, the break statement is
                   necessary so that the program won't
                   drop down into the next case. */
       case 3 : printf("Thirty "); break;
       case 4 : printf("Forty "); break;
       case 5 : printf("Fifty "); break;
       case 6 : printf("Sixty "); break;
       case 7 : printf("Seventy "); break;
       case 8 : printf("Eighty "); break;
       case 9 : printf("Ninety "); break;
```

```
      }
   }

void PrintWords( int num )
{
   /* Declare some local variables */
   int Hund, Tens;

   /* First, how many hundreds? */
   Hund = num / 100.0;
   if ( Hund > 0 )
   {
      PrintNum (Hund);
      printf("hundred ");
      /* Subtract the hundreds */
      num = num - (Hund * 100);
   }

   /* Now determine number of tens */
   Tens = num / 10.0;
   switch (Tens)
   {
      case 0 : break;  /* ignore zero! */
      case 1 :
         PrintTeen( (int) num );
         /* If a teen number was printed, no
            more work is required. */
         num = 0;
         break;
      default: /* for all the rest (2-9) */
         PrintTen( Tens );
         num = num - (Tens * 10);
         break;
   }

   /* Print the final number */
   if ( num > 0 ) PrintNum( (int) num );

}
```

The C solution, like the Pascal and BASIC solutions, is broken up into several routines. These are discussed next.

THE MAIN PROGRAM

Like BASIC, C requires you to define all your functions at the top of the program. This is done so that the compiler can check the functions and parameters as they are called throughout the program.

The main part of this program is rather simple. The name of the payee and the amount of the check are read from the user. The top part of the check is printed, and then the number of dollars and the number of cents are calculated, using the algorithms discussed earlier in this chapter. Finally, **PrintWords()** is called for both the dollar amount and the cents amounts.

The printing of the check amount uses the **printf()** function; it allows numbers to be printed with specific formatting. In this case, the format is

```
" %s   $%9.2f \n"
```

The **%s** symbol is used to print out the string value ("............"). The **$** places a dollar sign at the start of the number being printed. The **%9.2f** tells the **printf()** function that a floating point value should be expected, and that it should be printed in a field that is nine characters wide, with two characters following the decimal place. Here is an example of what this format would look like:

```
123456.89
```

Notice that the period takes up one of the nine positions.

Another oddity in C is the need to remove the carriage return from the user's input, which is read by the **fgets()** function. A carriage return (or line break) will occur whenever the user presses the ENTER key after typing an item of data.

There are two things you need to know about **fgets()**. First, **fgets()** is used instead of **scanf()** in this program to receive the entry of the payee's name. Why? Because **scanf()** stops reading text when it sees a space character. If the program used **scanf()**, and the user tried entering a first and last name, only the first name would be read, so only that name would be printed on the check. The **fgets()** function continues to read user input until the ENTER key is pressed, resulting in a line break.

Second, the carriage return entered by the user when he or she finishes typing becomes part of the string read by **fgets()**. Therefore, your program needs to delete that last character (the carriage return) from the string. This is done by determining the length of the string (using **strlen()**), and then replacing the appropriate character with a 0 character. (As you may recall, 0 terminates every

C string.) This makes the string one character shorter by overwriting the carriage return, making that position the new end of the string.

PrintNum()

This subroutine receives an integer and then prints the text name of that integer. In the Pascal solution, an array of words was used. A similar process is used here. Remember, however, that C arrays start with the number 0, not 1, so you need to subtract 1 from the parameter to select the correct word for printing.

PrintTeen()

This function receives an integer, assumed to be a number from 10 to 19; any other number will be ignored.

This could also be done with an array, but an additional calculation on the number would have to be made. For instance, if you stored the numbers in array elements 0 through 9, then in order to print the correct word you would need to subtract 10 from each number passed in.

PrintTen()

This function prints the correct multiple of 10, based on the parameter passed. It is nearly identical to **PrintTeen**, but prints a different set of names.

PrintWords()

The **PrintWords()** function performs most of the work in this program. It determines the number of hundreds, tens, and ones, according to the algorithms described earlier. It also determines if the tens and ones make a teen number.

Using the numbers calculated, the correct combination of **PrintNum**, **PrintTen**, and **PrintTeen** are called.

Selecting a Language (Reprise)

Now you have learned all that you can about real programming from a book of this type. You have seen how three of the most popular computer languages are used, and have examined an entire application developed in each of these languages. By now, you should have an idea which language *feels* best for you.

But before you go out and buy more books, or spend your money on compilers, language packages, and the like, read the next chapter. There, you will learn about the newest technologies and environments in software development; you'll also find out what features to look for as you start putting together your own development environment.

Chapter 8

New Development

Technologies

t H I S chapter will introduce some of the newer techniques being applied to the software development process, notably computer aided software engineering (CASE) tools and object-oriented programming (OOP) systems. It also gives you some ideas about the variety of development environments and programming tools that are available.

CASE Tools

Computer-aided software engineering is an attempt to bring the power of the computer into the development process used by programmers. With this method of programming, the software is designed on the computer, using graphical design tools, and the final programs are generated flawlessly. This, at least, is the goal. None of the CASE tools are this complete (yet!). But many of the functions that CASE tools provide are still highly desired by programmers.

Concepts of CASE

The most popular feature of CASE is its drawing utilities, or CASE Tools. CASE Tools allow a programmer to draw portions of a design, and then have them checked for consistency and accuracy.

Part of this systematic design process involves the building and maintenance of the *data dictionary*. The data dictionary is similar to any other dictionary; the names of all files, fields, and program modules in use by your design are stored there, with a short description, and often a physical location. In this way, you can quickly check that names are not duplicated incorrectly, and that each use of a specific name means the same thing throughout your design.

Another type of checking done by these programs is in drawing consistency. For instance, if you create a module on one drawing with two inputs and three outputs, this module must be the same in all other drawings.

Once your design is complete, many CASE tools will generate some or all of the required source code to match your design. For instance, it is common for CASE tools to first let you define your database layout, and then automatically generate the SQL commands necessary to create the database in your environment. (Your *database layout* specifies the files you will use for storing data, and the fields you will use within each file.)

The drawings that are used to generate this source code include Data Flow Diagrams (DFD), Function Hierarchy Diagrams (FHD), and Entity Relationship Diagrams (ERD). Of course, this is only a sampling of the diagram types available, but these are the ones used most.

Drawing Methods

There are three types of drawings that are most commonly used in CASE work, and supported by most CASE tools. These diagram types were introduced in Chapter 6; they are listed again here:

◆ **Data Flow Diagram (DFD)**   A DFD is used to portray the major functions that a system needs to perform, along with the connections between these functions. These connections are made up of the data elements being sent between the functions. If no information is passed between two functions, no connection is shown. A DFD does not try to show the flow of the program, or how the functions call each other; it only shows the data that is passed from one function to another, thus the name *Data Flow* Diagram. Figure 8-1 shows a sample DFD.

◆ **Function Hierarchy Diagram (FHD)**   An FHD is used to show the major functions in the system. Beneath each of the major functions are listed the subfunctions required for completion of the major function. This dissection of functions can continue indefinitely, with breakdowns shown of the smaller sub-subfunctions that are required by each subfunction. The purpose of these diagrams is to break the functionality down to a point where specific procedures can be written. You may recall that one of the steps of the design process is to break your program idea down into small steps; an FHD is an ideal way to depict that breakdown. Once your FHD is completed, coding can begin, and each of the objects at the lowest level of the FHD becomes a subroutine or function. Figure 8-2 shows a sample FHD.

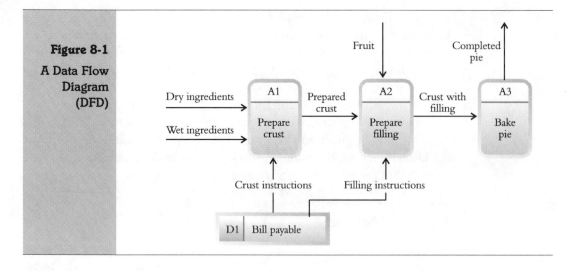

Figure 8-1

A Data Flow Diagram (DFD)

Entity Relationship Diagram (ERD) An ERD is used to graphically represent the program's database files and depict their relationships with each other. Figure 8-3 shows a sample ERD. Notice that each box in the drawing represents a single database file, Within each database, the fields within that file are shown. The fields that make up the unique nature of each record (that is, what makes that record different from all others in the file) are specially noted.

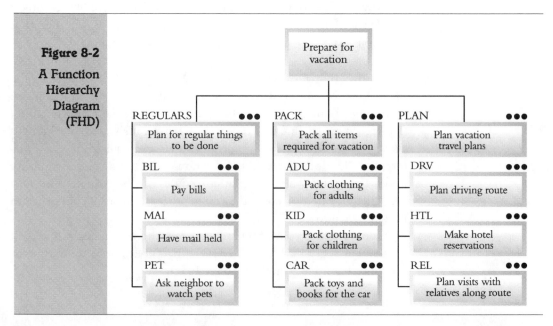

Figure 8-2

A Function Hierarchy Diagram (FHD)

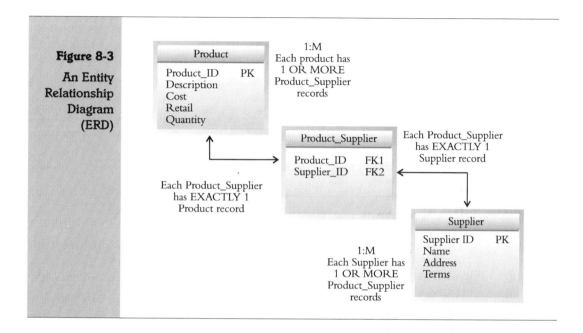

Figure 8-3

An Entity Relationship Diagram (ERD)

The connections that exist between database files are of three types: one-to-one, one-to-many, or many-to-many. *One-to-one* connections mean that for each record in one file, there will be exactly one related record in the other file. An example of this might be "Each record in the Personnel file has one and only one associated record in the AddressBook file."

A *one-to-many* connection means that for each record in one file, there will be one or more associated records in the other file. An example of this might be, "Each record in the Personnel file has one or more associated records in the PayCheck file."

A *many-to-many* relationship is one in which there are many records in one file that match many records in the other file. This may be difficult to understand, and the use of this type of relationship is not common for that reason; it is also difficult for more database programs to handle correctly. An example of this might be, "Many records in the Product file are related to each record in the Supplier file, but there are several records in the Supplier file for each record in the Product file."

Generally, if you find yourself with a many-to-many relationship, you should try to redesign your database to create one-to-many relationships instead. For instance, in the example above you could introduce a third file called Product_Supplier. The relationship would then become, "Each record in the Product file has one or more records in the Product_Supplier file, but each record in the Product_Supplier file points to only one record in the Product file. Likewise, each record in the Supplier file has one or more records in the Product_Supplier file, but each record in the Product_Supplier file points to only one record in the Supplier file." This is shown graphically in Figure 8-3.

Development Methodologies

To make things even more interesting, there are several different methodologies used in different schools of programming. As discussed in Chapter 6, a software development methodology prescribes the format of the drawings, and the steps used in the generation of the complete design. There are methodologies that support the type of programming you have been learning in this book, and others that are specific to event-driven or object-oriented programming (both discussed later in this chapter).

Several of the books listed in Appendix D deal specifically with different software development methodologies. Before choosing one for yourself, consider how each methodology is defined: the types of programs that can be designed, the types of drawings that are used, and the support available from CASE programs.

caution: *Keep in mind that many software development methodologies are not completely (or correctly) supported by the CASE tools. Make sure that the tool you select fully supports your chosen methodology, or else choose a different methodology that is fully supported. Otherwise, you'll end up preparing some of your diagrams by hand, and you'll lose the advantages—such as consistency checks and data dictionary maintenance—that come with using an automated tool.*

While standard methodologies are all suitable for most design work, the best methodology is one that works for you. Often, you will be forced to work with a methodology that is already in place in your workplace. Fear not; most of these methodologies only differ in their diagram formats. If you are given the opportunity to make a choice, send for demonstration disks from the vendors of several CASE tools. Then make a selection based on their features, as well as their availability on your platform of choice.

Object-Oriented Programming

Object-oriented programming has been around for a number of years, but only recently have its tools been made available for the average programmer. And while OOP is a wonderful tool, it requires a basic change in thought patterns. Using OOP means learning to design your programs around the objects involved (that is, around the individual subroutines), instead of focusing on a global knowledge of the entire process.

note: *Object-oriented programming can be thought of as a bottom-up procedure, as opposed to more traditional, top-down programming.*

What are objects? Simply the things you deal with each day in real life. Objects are not something designed just for programmers. Take a moment and think of the objects you are using as you read this book. The book is an object, as is the chair you are sitting in, your house, the can of diet soda sitting next to you, and the lamp shining on this page.

Relating these objects to programming involves a change in thought patterns from more traditional structured programming concepts. Previously, programmers thought about data and about functions that would process data. With OOP, a programmer must define everything in terms of the object at hand: how the object will act, what data it knows about itself, and how it reacts with objects around it. Once you make this paradigm shift, you will be able to create reusable objects that will greatly simplify and speed up your future programming.

Computer Lingo

A *paradigm* is simply a way of thinking, a type of thought pattern. A *paradigm shift* is what happens when you are required to change your way of thinking; you are forced to shift to another way of thinking. For instance, a widespread paradigm shift occurred when Columbus came back and reported that the world is round, and not flat. Another major paradigm shift took place when scientists discovered that the Earth is *not* the center of the universe.

Concepts of OOP

There are three basic concepts that an object-oriented language or environment must support: polymorphism, encapsulation, and inheritance.

POLYMORPHISM

The basis of *polymorphism* is being able to name like items with the same name. For instance, even though Jill, Jim, and Jack are different people, they all have something called a nose. It would be silly to call their noses a Jill_Nose, a Jim_Nose, and a Jack_Nose. In fact, in real life it would be absurd.

With OOP, you want to have this same ability to assign like items the same name, and allow the context of the situation determine which of the numerous items to use. For instance, you may write a procedure that determines the absolute value of a number. Without polymorphism, you will need at least three different copies of this routine to be able to handle all types of numbers; in C, their prototypes might look like this:

```
int   Abs_Int( int num );
long  Abs_Long( long num );
float Abs_Float( float num );
```

With polymorphism, you can assign all three of the functions in this example (**Abs_Int**, **Abs_Long**, and **Abs_Float**) the same name. The compiler will decide which one to call based on the parameter type passed in when the function is called. In C++, these same three functions, now all named the same thing, might be prototyped in this way:

```
int   Abs( int num );
long  Abs( long num );
float Abs( float num );
```

ENCAPSULATION

Encapsulation, also known as data hiding, is the ability to gather, and optionally hide, the data within an object. For example, you probably own or use a television set—but you probably don't open the set and poke around with the insides of it too often. There is probably a sticker that warns "Only Qualified Technicians Should Open this Television for Service." This is a type of encapsulation. You can use your TV without knowing what is inside of it. The set may use tubes, resisters, or digital signal processing, but as long as the on/off button works, you probably don't know or care what is inside. Everything the TV needs in order to operate, though, is contained within its plastic confines.

Programming objects, which are really just individual functions or routines, are also self-contained. You need to know how to use them, but their internal operations, or how they work, are only important to the original developer. Objects are made up of two parts—data and methods. Data is the information available to the object (its current state). Methods are commands that the object understands. For instance, your TV knows how to be turned on and off. Here is a simplified C++ object for a television set:

```
class Television
{
  // First define the items that do not
  // need to be seen from the outside
  private:

    // These data elements are not even known
    // outside of the television
    int tubes;
    int wires;
    int transistors;

    // These data elements are maintained inside
    // the television, but can be changed and
    // viewed using the public methods

    int CurrentChannel;
    int VolumeLevel;
    int TintLevel;
    int ContrastLevel;

  // Now the items that CAN be seen:
  public:

    // Now the methods to make changes
    void TurnOn();
    void TurnOff();
    void ChangeChannel();
    void ChangeVolume();
    void ChangeTint();
    void ChangeContrast();
```

```
// Method to display current settings
void DisplayCurrentInfo();

// Methods to request specific information
int ChannelIs();
int VolumeLevelIs();
int TintLevelIs();
int ContrastLevelIs();
}
```

Within an object, the data and methods can be private (the transistors that are installed in the TV, the details of how the power supply is connected to the circuit board, etc.), or public (the current channel selected, the on/off command, etc.). The private information is used by the object to maintain its current state of processing, and is not available to other objects. The public information is used by other objects to give commands to the object in question, or to determine its current state.

You may notice in the television object described above that the actual data is not accessible outside the object; it is all in the private section of the class definition. Why? You don't want anyone changing this information without using the right methods (pun intended). This would be like going inside the TV and manually changing the channel; the display on the front of the set would then be incorrect. Encapsulation is not just for hiding data—it is also for protecting data! As you can see in the sample code above, you the programmer need to supply methods for setting and checking the current value of each data element in use. In this way, *you* define how the data can be changed.

INHERITANCE

One of the great benefits of object-oriented programming is its ability to reuse the code and objects created in previous programs. Inheritance is the method by which much of this recycling occurs.

Inheritance means that data and methods from one class of objects can be passed on to a new class, without the need for redefining all of the information. Perhaps an example will help your understanding of this concept.

In grade school, you may have played a game called "20 Questions." In this game, the goal is to discover what object is in someone else's mind. Often, the first question is something like, "Is it animal, vegetable, or mineral?" While this is a simplified classification of all the objects in the world, let's start with these as our "base classes," from which all other objects will inherit traits. Figure 8-4 illustrates this idea.

Figure 8-4

A graphical 20 questions

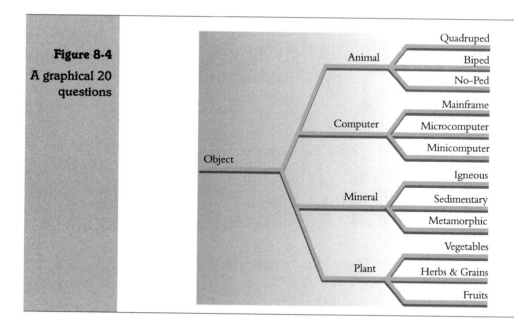

Even in this school-age game, players generally have the knowledge that animals have some common characteristics. Animals are alive, they can move, they have offspring. Vegetables, on the other hand, cannot move, and they live at least partially underground. Minerals are not alive, cannot move, and do not bear young.

When you ask the next question, you know some basic characteristics about all animals, so the next goal is to find the "subclass" of the object. For instance, some animals have two legs, some have four, and others move on their bellies. Inheritance allows you to break this knowledge down one step at a time (as shown in Figure 8-5), and to know that characteristics of the parent class still exist for the subclasses.

Assuming that the final object is a kitten, you know that it has four legs, because its parent class (Quadruped) has that characteristic. In addition, you know that it is alive, can move, and can have offspring, because those characteristics are inherited from the "animal" class.

Therefore, when you describe your kitten to someone, there is no need to explain how many legs it has, or that it is alive. This information is assumed because of the inheritance from the parent classes.

Your specific kitten is called an "instance" of the kitten class. It has all the characteristics of a standard kitten, which makes it like all other kittens. You know, for instance, that it has fur, eyes, and paws. As an instance, you can give actual values to each of the characteristics. Not only does your kitten have fur

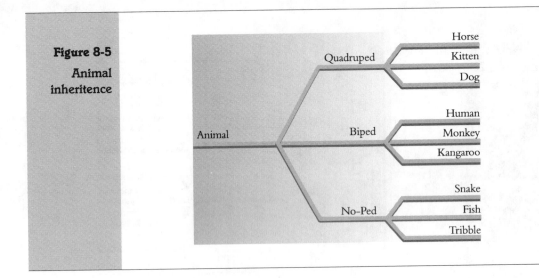

Figure 8-5

Animal inheritance

Animal

Quadruped — Horse, Kitten, Dog

Biped — Human, Monkey, Kangaroo

No-Ped — Snake, Fish, Tribble

(as do all kittens), but the color of its hair is grey (its own value). Your kitten has eyes (as do all kittens), with the specific color of blue (its own value).

A Popular OOP Language—C++

The overview of objects and classes presented above doesn't give you much of a feel for object-oriented programming. It may not even seem to pertain to programming at all. This is why many people refer to object-oriented programming as a paradigm shift; it involves a fundamental difference in how you think about programming.

Instead of designing software with a broad, global understanding of everything involved with the project, you now start by thinking about the actual objects that will be involved, and how they will interact. For many people, this is a difficult change in focus; however, once you make the transition, you'll have a much easier time creating code that can be reused in many projects to come.

note: *As a beginning programmer, you are actually at a great advantage here! If you don't have a lot of experience with more traditional methods of program development, then you haven't developed any rigid ideas or habits that might prevent you from approaching newer methods, such as object-oriented programming, with an open mind.*

The next step is to show you how these concepts are used in a programming environment, and how they extend to your own programming capabilities. C++ will be used to demonstrate these concepts; C++ is an object-oriented "upgrade" to C, and it allows for the concepts of polymorphism, encapsulation, and inheritance.

CREATING CLASSES AND OBJECTS

C++ introduces a new keyword, *class,* that is used to create objects. Classes are similar to C structures, but include both data and functions. In fact, **struct**'s in C++ can even hold functions. The data and functions in a **struct** or **class** have one of three designations, determining what access to that item is available:

◆ *Public* items can be viewed (data) or called (functions) by any other function or object. Public items are preceded by the keyword **public:** in C++.

◆ *Protected* items can be viewed or called by other objects of the same type, or of any type that inherits from the object in question. Protected items are preceded by the keyword **protected:** in C++.

◆ *Private* items cannot be viewed or called by any other objects or functions. These items are totally internal to the object, and are preceded by the keyword **private:** in C++.

The only difference between a **class** and a **struct** (in C++) is that everything in a **struct** is considered public by default, and everything in a **class** is considered private by default. However, you can always use **private:**, **public:**, and **protected:** to override the defaults. In fact, the following declarations are all equivalent.

▬▬▬▬

***struct* with No Defaults** This example shows the use of a **struct**, rather than a **class**. However, all items are denoted as either private or public, so no defaults are assumed. The items following **private:** cannot be accessed outside of this object, while the items following **public:** will be accessible from other objects or functions.

```
// This structure specifies each section
// as private or public.
struct aPerson
{
```

```
    private:
        int age;
        int weight;
        char *name;
    public:
        float height;
        // Constructor is next:
        aPerson( char *Name, int Wt, float Ht, int Age );
        // Now a destructor:
        ~aPerson();
        // Other functions
        void SayName();        // prototype
        void TellAboutMe();    // prototype
};
```

A struct with Defaults The following example shows the use of a **struct**, where the first few items default to public access. This happens because a **struct** is all public by default. The items following the keyword **private:** cannot be viewed by other objects.

```
// This structure specifies the private section, and allows
// other areas to default to public.
struct aPerson
{
    float height;
    aPerson( char *Name, int Wt, float Ht, int Age );
    ~aPerson();
    void SayName();        // prototype
    void TellAboutMe();    // prototype
  private:
    int age;
    int weight;
    char *name;
};
```

A class with No Defaults This example shows the use of a **class** where all items are denoted as either private or public; no defaults are assumed. The items following **private:** cannot be accessed outside of this object, while the items following **public:** will be accessible from other objects or functions.

```
// This class specifies all sections as private or public.
class aPerson
{
  private:
     int age;
     int weight;
     char *name;
  public:
     float height;
     aPerson( char *Name, int Wt, float Ht, int Age );
     ~aPerson();
     void SayName();      // prototype
     void TellAboutMe();  // prototype
};
```

___

A class with Defaults The following example shows the use of a **class**, where the first few items default to private access. This happens because a **class** is all private by default. However, the items following the keyword **public:** can be viewed by other objects.

```
// This class specifies the public section, and allows
// other areas to default to private.
class aPerson
{
     int age;
     int weight;
     char *name;
  public:
     float height;
     aPerson( char *Name, int Wt, float Ht, int Age );
     ~aPerson();
     void SayName();      // prototype
     void TellAboutMe();  // prototype
};
```

MORE ABOUT WRITING CLASSES

Once you have defined your classes, you need to write the functions that appear within each class. To implement the **SayName()** function in the class above, you would write the following code:

```
aPerson::SayName()
{
    printf("My name is %s\n", name);
}
```

To write the functions specified in the **class** or **struct** definition, a scope resolution operator (::) is used (as shown in the preceding example). This operator tells the compiler that the function being written is to be associated with the class preceding the operator. (In this example, the class is **aPerson**, and the function is **SayName()**.)

A class may have two special functions, known as the constructor and destructor. The *constructor* is a function that is called automatically when the object is created; it has the same name as the object. The *destructor* is a function that is called automatically when the object is destroyed; it has the same name as the constructor, but preceeded with the ~ (tilde) character. For example, the following class has both a constructor and destructor defined:

```
class aPerson
{
    int age;
    int weight;
    char *name;
 public:
    float height;
    aPerson( char *Name, int Wt,        ┐
            float Ht, int Age );─┘         ──── Constructor
    ~aPerson();                   ◄───────────── Destructor
    void SayName();        // prototype
    void TellAboutMe();    // prototype
};
```

There are two rules that must be followed in creating constructors and destructors.

1. A constructor cannot have a return value. However, one or more parameters may be sent to the constructor. In fact, multiple constructors can be created, each with a different set of parameters.

2. A destructor cannot have a return value or any parameters. Destructors are called without any programmer intervention, so there is no way to send in parameters. Also, there can be only one destructor for each object.

The following example shows a complete implementation using this class, including the constructor, the destructor, and the use of variables of the **aPerson** class type.

```cpp
// Program to demonstrate the use of a class
// File:      Person.CPP
// Author:    L. John Ribar
// Date:      8 Oct 1995
// System:    C++

#include <stdio.h>      // allows use of i/o
#include <string.h>     // string handling

// Define the aPerson class
class aPerson
{
    int age;
    int weight;
    char *name;
  public:
    float height;
    aPerson( char *Name, int Wt, float Ht, int Age );
    ~aPerson();
    void SayName();       // prototype
    void TellAboutMe();   // prototype
};

// Now the main program

void main()
{
    // This is where the object instances are
    // defined.  This is where the constructor is
    // actually called, and where the parameters
    // are passed in for processing. However,
    // these are really just variable declarations,
    // so the variables Mary and John will be
    // available throughout the main program.
    aPerson Mary( "Mary", 138, 62.5, 26 );
    aPerson John( "John", 220, 73, 31 );

    printf("Here are the names of the people: \n");
    Mary.SayName();
    John.SayName();
```

```
    printf("Here are the statistics about Mary:\n ");
    Mary.TellAboutMe();

    printf("Here are the statistics about John:\n ");
    John.TellAboutMe();
}

// This is the constructor. This is called when a
// variable of this type is declared or allocated.
// This is where the internal details are assigned.
aPerson::aPerson( char *Name, int Wt, float Ht, int Age )
{
    name = new char[ strlen(Name) + 1 ];    // allocate space
    strcpy( name, Name );                    // save the name
    weight = Wt;                             // and the other
details
    age = Age;
    height = Ht;

    // This will let you see where the object is actually
    // initialized.
    printf("Created %s \n", name);
}

// This is the destructor. It is called when a variable of
this
// type goes out of scope.
aPerson::~aPerson()
{
    // This lets you see where the variable goes out of scope
    printf("Destroying %s \n", name);

    delete name;         // release the space allocated
}

void aPerson::SayName()
{
    printf("%s \n", name);
}

void aPerson::TellAboutMe()
{
```

```
    printf("Hello. My name is %s. I am %d \n",
        name, age );
    printf("year old, weight %d pounds and am about \n",
        weight);
    printf("%f inches tall.\n", height );
}
```

Running this program would display the following results. Notice where the constructor and destructor print their messages!

```
Created Mary
Created John
Here are the names of the people:
Mary
John
Here are the statistics about Mary:
Hello. My name is Mary. I am 26
years old, weigh 138 pounds, and am about
62.5 inches tall.
Here are the statistics about John:
Hello. My name is John. I am 31
years old, weigh 220 pounds, and am about
73 inches tall.
Destroying John
Destroying Mary
```

Now that you have seen an object at work, it's time that you explore the true strength of object-oriented programming. In the following section, you'll see how the concepts of encapsulation, polymorphism, and inheritance are handled in C++.

ENCAPSULATION—HIDING THE INTERNALS

In a C++ class, everything is considered private unless it is specified otherwise. This means that, by default, no other programs, routines, or variables have access to the information in the class. This is greatly different from a C struct, where everyone has access to any member of the structure, and where that data can be changed at any time.

Some things cannot remain hidden, however. If you want to be able to use a class, there must be commands that you can give it, and these commands must be public. Therefore, C++ uses the **private:** and **public:** keywords to note which portions of the class are available.

There is also a third keyword, **protected:**, that is used in objects. Protected variables and functions can be used by other objects of the same class, or by any of its subclasses. Elsewhere, protected items are considered private.

Why is encapsulation important? It allows you to write code and use variables that have very strict access. No other parts of your program can have access to these variables and functions unless you specifically say they can. This level of control greatly simplifies debugging, because you know exactly what parts of each object can be changed by any code other than the code within the object itself.

POLYMORPHISM—REWRITING THE RULES

Polymorphism allows multiple functions to have the same name. This feature helps make your programs more readable, and simplifies the programming process itself. Once you've taken advantage of polymorphism, you don't have to remember whether the print routine for long integers is called **lPrint()**, **longPrint()**, **LongPrint()**, **PrintLong()**, or some other name; all print routines can be called **Print()**, and the parameters you pass in will determine the specific routine that will be used.

Polymorphism is especially useful when used with classes. For example, suppose that you want to create a window class for use on your computer screen. Its prototype might look something like this:

```
class Window
{
   int topRow, leftCol;       // top left corner position
   int Rows, Cols;            // window size
   int ForeColor, BackColor;  // colors to use
   int Border;                // border type
                              // 0 = none, 1 = single, 2 =
double
  public:
   Window();         // default is a full screen window, no
border
   Window( int top, int left, int rows, int cols, int
border=1);
   void SetColor( int Fore );
   void SetColor( int Fore, int Back );
};
```

Examine the class definition above, and you can see where polymorphism can simplify your programming tasks. There are two constructors, each named

Window. One of these constructors allows a default window to be built, and therefore requires no parameters. The other allows for the position and size to be specified.

Notice that the variable **border** is given a value in the prototype for **Window()**! In C++, you can assign default values to parameters. The parameters that get defaults, however, must be at the end of the parameter list. In other words, the compiler has to have some way of knowing what order the parameters are in.

In the example above, the default **border** value allows the function to be called with either four or five parameters. If called with four, **border** takes on the default value of 1, as specified in the prototype. Otherwise, the value passed in when the function is called will be used. By the way, the default value is only shown in the prototype, not in the actual code you write for the function.

The two versions of **SetColor()** allow for either the foreground or both the foreground and background colors to be selected, depending on how the function is called. You could use a single function with default values to set both colors, like this:

```
void SetColor( int Fore, int Back = -1 );
```

In this case, the code for **SetColor()** would have to check for a value of -1 for the background color. This could be your signal that no change should be made to the background color. By writing the code this way, you eliminate the need for an extra function altogether!

Deciding whether to use default values or numerous polymorphic functions is partially a matter of personal preference, and partially determined by the use of the function. If combining two routines and using an extra (default) parameter will result in a more compact, efficient routine, then you might choose to use default values. If the functions require different types of parameters, and process them in different ways, then using numerous functions with the same name will probably be the better choice.

Polymorphism exists even in the C language, but you cannot make any changes to it. For instance, the **+** operator is used for addition of integers, longs, floats, doubles and characters. Think what problems programmers would have if addition required a different operator for each type of variable! The difference in C++ is that you can add functionality to **+**, and most other operators, for your own structures and classes—a level of flexibility that C does not allow.

For instance, if you create your own data types, C will not allow you to add them together using the **+** operator. C++, on the other hand, does allow you to create a new operation, called **+**, that works specifically for your new data type. And **+** is not the only operator that can be defined; **+, -, /, *, [ ], ++,** **− −,** and others can be defined in C++.

INHERITANCE—BUILDING ON A SOLID FOUNDATION

Inheritance allows you to create a base class, and use the information within it to generate new classes, without repeating the work you have already done. An example might help here!

Suppose you are designing a screen management class. You might create such functions as writing to the screen, reading from the keyboard, and saving the contents of the screen into a file. Later, if you want to create a window management class, you can reuse the functions from your screen management class, adding the capability to draw a border (window) around a portion of the screen. Other features provided by the screen class could be used unchanged. Here is the concept as it might look in code:

```
class Screen
{
    char image[4000];       // PC text screen
  public:
    Screen();               // constructor
    WriteAt( int row, int col, char c);
    WriteAt( int row, int col, char *s);
    WriteAt( int row, int col, int i);
    Erase();                // clear screen
    Erase( int r1, int c1, int r2, int c2 );  // clear portion
};

class Window : public Screen     // inherit Screen class
{
    int top, left, bottom, right;
  public:
    Window();   // default to full screen
    Window( int r1, int c1, int r2, int c2 );
    Clear();    // clear the window
};
```

After these declarations, a Window object can use any of the functions already created for Screen objects. For instance, the **Window::Clear()** function might be as simple as this:

```
Window::Clear()
{
   // Erase area between the borders
   Erase( top+1, left+1, bottom-1, right-1 );
}
```

You may notice that you've written this function without even knowing how the Screen class is implemented! And because the Window class inherits the Screen class, all the functions, like **Erase()**, are available without any special scope resolution operators.

This has been a quick introduction to object-oriented programming with C++. You will probably want to look at some of the reference guides listed in Appendix D for more detailed conceptual training. C++ is not the only language used for OOP. Other popular languages include Smalltalk and Borland Pascal with Objects.

Smalltalk is a *pure* object-oriented programming language. This means that all programming in Smalltalk revolves around the objects. In C++, the procedural programming capabilities of C have not been abandoned, so it gives you the option of programming without using objects.

Borland Pascal with Objects is the latest incarnation of Turbo Pascal; among the added features are OOP capabilities. This version of Pascal is implemented in a manner similar to C++: You can continue to use your existing, structured code, and add objects as you want or need to.

Graphical User Interfaces (GUIs) and Event-Driven Programming

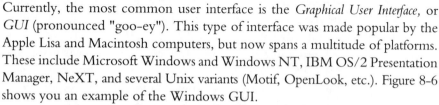

Currently, the most common user interface is the *Graphical User Interface,* or GUI (pronounced "goo-ey"). This type of interface was made popular by the Apple Lisa and Macintosh computers, but now spans a multitude of platforms. These include Microsoft Windows and Windows NT, IBM OS/2 Presentation Manager, NeXT, and several Unix variants (Motif, OpenLook, etc.). Figure 8-6 shows you an example of the Windows GUI.

Graphical interfaces provide yet another paradigm shift for the programmer, but are much more akin to OOP design than to structured, sequential coding. This relationship is a result of how the interface works. A GUI is a program itself, which handles all input from and output to the user. Therefore, your program must be able to receive messages from the GUI itself, recognizing when one or more GUI commands have occurred. These commands might

Figure 8-6

Microsoft
Windows: A
popular GUI

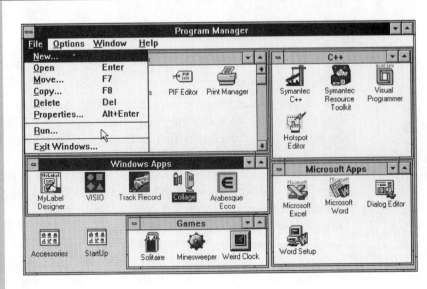

include menu selections, moving or sizing of windows, or drawing within a window. In every case, your program must know how to handle the message.

This activity is quite different from that of non–GUI programs, in which a programmer dictates the order in which a program is executed. With GUIs, you never know when a user will move a window, or change its size. Even in the midst of printing a report, the user might decide to cancel it, and start a different task. So your programs must be much more aware of all the things that *might* happen, and must have a plan for anything the user might do.

This type of programming is called *event-driven* programming. The program is driven, or caused to act, by external events. These events usually come from the user, but may also come from the GUI program, a serial port, or another program that is running at the same time.

Here is an example of a program written for Microsoft Windows. Naturally, this program would not actually do much, but it does illustrate how event-driven programming is implemented. It also shows the use of Hungarian notation, which you learned about in Chapter 4.

```
/*
    Simple Windows Program to say Hello.
*/
```

```c
#include <windows.h>

/* Prototypes */
LONG FAR PASCAL EventHandler( HWND, UINT,
                              WPARAM, LPARAM);


/* Global variables */
char szProgramName[] = "Hello";

/*
    The WinMain() function is required in every Windows
    program. It replaces the main() function found in
    normal C programs. WinMain() defines the way that
    the program should look, and then goes into a loop,
    which receives messages from Windows and processes
    them.
*/
int PASCAL WinMain( HINSTANCE hInst, HINSTANCE pInst,
          LPSTR lpszCommandLine, int nCommandShow );
{
    HWND hWnd;
    MSG  lpMsg;
    WNDCLASS wcMyApp;

    if (!pInst)
    {
        wcMyApp.lpszClassName = szProgramName;
        wcMyApp.hInstance = hInst;
        wcMyApp.lpfnWndProc = EventHandler;
        wcMyApp.hCursor = LoadCursor(NULL,IDC_ARROW);
        wcMyApp.hIcon = NULL;
        wcMyApp.lpszMenuName = NULL;
        wcMyApp.hbrBackground = GetStockObject(WHITE_BRUSH);
        wcMyApp.style = CS_HREDRAW | CS_VREDRAW;
        wcMyApp.cbClsExtra = 0;
        wcMyApp.cbWndExtra = 0;
        if (!RegisterClass( &wcMyApp ))
            return FALSE;
    }
    hWnd = CreateWindow( szProgramName, "Hello There!",
                WS_OVERLAPPEDWINDOW, CW_USEDEFAULT,
            CW_USEDEFAULT, CW_USEDEFAULT, CW_USEDEFAULT,
```

```
                        (HWND)NULL, (HMENU)NULL, (HANDLE)hInst,
                                           (LPSTR)NULL );
      ShowWindow( hWnd, nCommandShow );
      UpdateWindow( hWnd );

      /* Here is the main processing loop. */
      while ( GetMessage( &lpMsg, NULL, NULL, NULL) )
      {
         TranslateMessage( &lpMsg );
         DispatchMessage( &lpMsg );
      }

      return ( lpMsg.wParam );
   }

/*
   Here is the meat of the program, where the events
   that occur will be handled. If this were a larger
   program, with more features, there would be many
   more entries in the switch statement below!
*/
LONG PAR PASCAL EventHandler( HWND hWnd, UINT msg,
                  WPARAM wParam, LPARAM lParam )
{
   PAINTSTRUCT ps;
   HDC hdc;

   switch (msg)
   {
      case WM_PAINT:
         hdc = BeginPaint( hWnd, &ps );
         /* this is where you would put commands
            to place text or graphics into your
            window */
         ValidateRect( hWnd, NULL );
         EndPaint( hWnd, &ps );
         break;
      case WM_DESTROY:
         PostQuitMessage(0);
         break;
      default:
         /* If this program does not handle a specific
```

```
          event (or message), pass it to the default
          Windows message handler, as shown here. */
       return( DefWindowProc( hWnd, msg,
                    wParam, lParam ));
   }

   return (0L);
}
```

Selecting a Development Environment

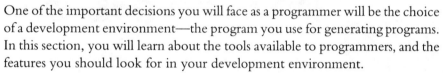

One of the important decisions you will face as a programmer will be the choice of a development environment—the program you use for generating programs. In this section, you will learn about the tools available to programmers, and the features you should look for in your development environment.

Many programmers develop their environments as a collection of separate programs, used together to edit, compile, debug, and test their programs. For many years, in fact, this kind of setup was a programmer's only choice. More recently, however, compiler vendors have been adding integrated environments to their products, allowing many of what were previously separate tools to be available directly from within their environments.

Tools You Will Want to Have

There are several tools you will want to have in your environment, whether as integrated or separate programs. These tools include editors, debuggers, revision control packages, and user interface designers.

PROGRAMMERS' EDITORS

Most language vendors now supply editors, which are the programs that allow you to enter and edit your own programs. Usually, these editors will have direct ties into the compiler, so that you can immediately compile your code once it is written. Figure 8-7 shows you the text-based program editor packaged with Borland's C++ compiler. (There is also a Windows-based editor.)

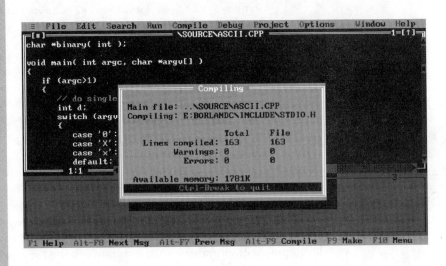

Figure 8-7

Borland's text-based environment

Computer Lingo

A programmers' editor is a type of word processor designed specifically for computer programmers. Instead of allowing the selection of formatting options, fonts, and other features designed to enhance the aesthetics of a document, a programmers' editor is more likely to provide a function that matches the braces in C, for example, or the **BEGIN** and **END** statements in Pascal. (These functions would help you to find the beginning and end of large pieces of code, and to make sure that the pairs are correctly matched.) Program editors can also be used for many word processing tasks.

There are several excellent editors, written specifically for programmers, that are available from non-compiler companies. If you plan to use several compilers, one of these third-party editors might be a good bet; they allow you to access several compilers without learning the different editing commands for each one.

As an example, one of the most popular programmers' editors available for use on the PC is called Brief; it is currently sold by Borland International. You can configure Brief to directly call your programming tools of choice, based on the extension of the file you are editing. So you could call the Borland C++ compiler for C and CPP files, Borland Pascal for PAS files, Microsoft

FORTRAN for FOR files, and Realia COBOL for COB files. In addition, Brief includes a complete facility for adding your own commands, which you write in a language based on C. These commands are then available within the editor, just as if they were original elements of the program. Brief will also automatically indent your code according to the language you are using, which results in cleaner code listings. Brief is not the only editor available of this magnitude; it is described here as an example to show you the type of power available. The Brief editor is shown in Figure 8-8.

Standard word processors often cannot be used for entering program code because of the unique way that they store files. These files often include special characters used to denote font selections, formatting options, and the like. Compilers expect what is commonly referred to as a *pure ASCII file*. This is a file that contains only the letters, numbers, and special characters used in programming. If you must use a word processor for editing your programs, be sure to save the file in ASCII format; most word processors provide this option.

DEBUGGERS

Many compilers now come with some level of debugger. There are three major types of debuggers: a static debugger, a run-time debugger, and a postmortem debugger.

Figure 8-8

Brief: A Programmers' Editor

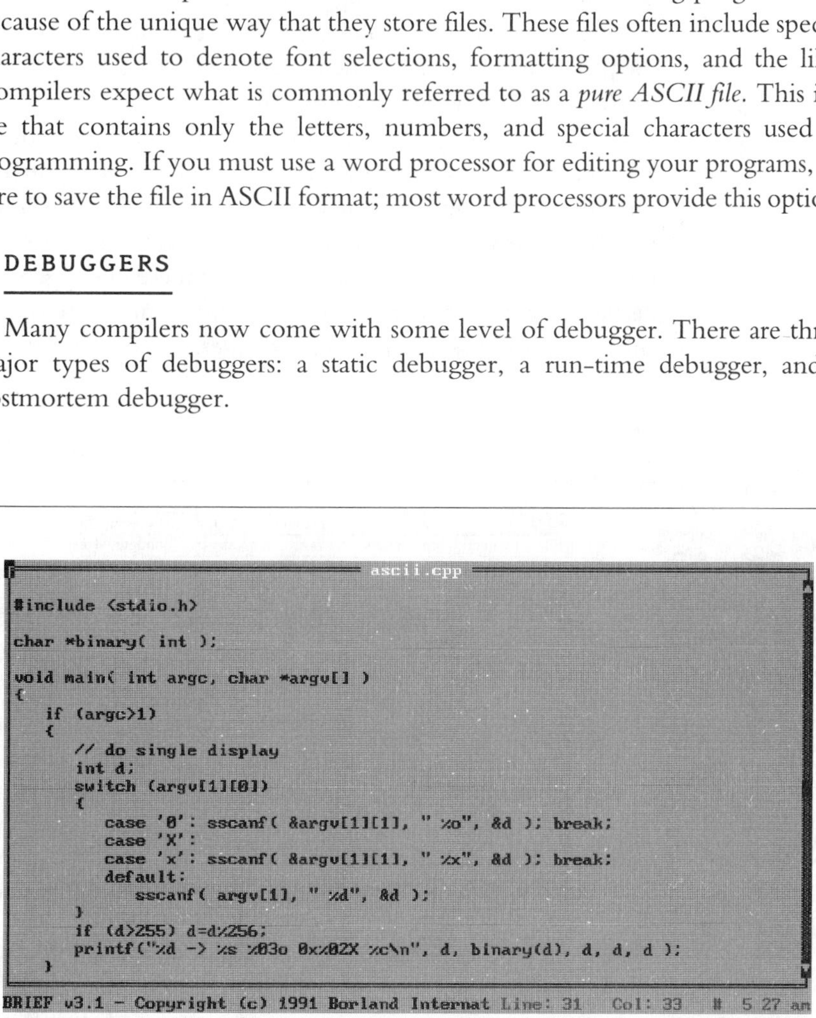

```
                          ══ ascii.cpp ═════════════
#include <stdio.h>

char *binary( int );

void main( int argc, char *argv[] )
{
    if (argc>1)
    {
        // do single display
        int d;
        switch (argv[1][0])
        {
        case '0': sscanf( &argv[1][1], " %o", &d ); break;
        case 'X':
        case 'x': sscanf( &argv[1][1], " %x", &d ); break;
        default:
            sscanf( argv[1], " %d", &d );
        }
        if (d>255) d=d%256;
        printf("%d -> %s %03o 0x%02X %c\n", d, binary(d), d, d, d );
    }
```

BRIEF v3.1 - Copyright (c) 1991 Borland Internat Line: 31   Col: 33   # 5 27 am

Computer Lingo

A *debugger* is a special program that allows you to watch what happens as your program executes. Symbolic debuggers show you the actual lines of your program as they execute.

A *static debugger* only allows you to view information at *break points,* special places in your program where you have designated that you would like the program to stop. The debugger will stop at these points, and you can look at the current value of variables, and the state of the program. You then restart the program, and wait for the next break point. Some debuggers also allow you to change values while the program is stopped.

A *run-time debugger* allows you to step through your source code, one line at a time, without setting specific break points. As you come upon calls to subroutines or functions, you can either follow the program into these routines, watching every step within them, or just allow the routine to execute and then return to your next line of code. Most of these debuggers also allow a dynamic display of variables; the variables and their values are displayed in a window, and are updated as the program executes.

Figure 8-9

Symantec's debugging tool for C++

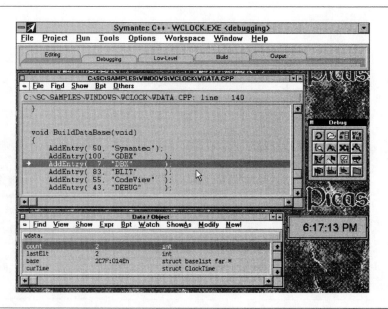

A *postmortem debugger* (PMD) is often used when your program crashes for no apparent reason. You cannot watch the execution of the program with a PMD, but special code in the program will write out a special *dump file* when the program ends. (This special code must be added to your program, but is usually supplied with the PMD. It only requires that your program be rebuilt; no change to the actual source code is necessary.) The dump file is then viewed with the postmortem debugger. The PMD allows you to see what was happening in the program when it stopped working. Usually, you will be able to see the value of each variable, as well as which line of code the program stopped on, and what sequence of function calls were made to get to that line of code.

Microsoft and Borland now provide full source-level debugging at the run-time level with their compilers. Microsoft CodeView and Borland TDebug are each available for use across the entire line of compilers available from each vendor. In this way, you only need to master one debugger if you stick to one vendor. In addition, multilanguage projects can be debugged under a single program.

Symantec provides both run-time and postmortem debugging facilities in their C++ compiler environment. Other compiler vendors provide some level of support for debugging, often including static debugging and a link to either CodeView or TDebug. Figure 8-9 shows Symantec's C++ debugging utility.

There are also third-party products available for debugging. For instance, Symantec's MultiScope Debuggers, available for DOS and Windows, support a wide variety of compilers, and provide both run-time and postmortem debugging. As with editors, if you plan to work with multiple compiler vendors and languages, a debugger that works with a greater variety of compilers will keep you from having to learn multiple tools.

REVISION CONTROL

Revision control programs are available on many different platforms, including DOS, Windows, Unix, Vax/VMS, and more. In fact, revision control tools are probably available on nearly every platform, in one form or another.

Computer Lingo

R*evision control* tools are used to track the different revisions of your program source code that occur as your project evolves.

Revision control provides several benefits:

1. You can always recall a previous version of a file if a change you make doesn't work out as planned.

2. You can pull out the specific versions of a file that was used with a specific program release. This can be very useful in program maintenance.

3. If you comment each revision of a file with the reasons that changes were made, you can quickly document the types of changes that were required, when they were made, and by whom.

4. Finally, all the source code revisions are stored in a central location, making backup simpler (and making it more difficult to find an excuse NOT to do your backups!). Also, in a team programming environment, you can be assured that only one programmer will have a file at a time. This prevents changes from being made by two programmers at the same time, in the same file.

This is how revision control works. As you complete a piece of code, or at least complete a portion of the code, you will *check in* the code. This makes a copy of your latest version, and tracks the author, date, and nature of the change. You then *check out* the code to continue working with it, if necessary. Most revision control packages will allow you to perform an *audit check-in,* which is a check-in and check-out performed simultaneously for all the files you plan to keep working with.

There are two storage methods used with the common revision control packages: *gamma storage* and *delta storage.* Gamma storage maintains a complete copy of each file you check in, and each revision of the file. This is somewhat faster than delta storage, but uses much more disk storage.

Delta storage only stores the latest revision of each file, along with the changes necessary for recreating the previous versions. Therefore, checking files in and out of a delta system takes some processing time, but results in much smaller storage files.

Some of the more common revision control programs include sccs (source code control system) and rcs (revision control system), available on most Unix systems; PVCS, from Intersolv, available on DOS, Windows, Unix, and many other platforms; and Microsoft Delta and Omega Systems versions, available for the Windows platform. If you plan to work on multiple platforms, look into a package like PVCS that is available on most platforms. If you only plan to work with Unix, sccs should work for you.

USER INTERFACE DESIGNERS

There are now a great number of programming tools that are used to help design your user interface. Borland, Microsoft, and Symantec all provide tools for the design of Windows front-ends. Third parties provide tools for designing text and Windows based user interfaces.

Most of the user interface designers allow you to draw a screen for your user, and then generate the source code you will need for your program to actually use the screen.

Design tools are often very specific to a compiler or library. There are some third party tools that allow you to design a screen once, and then use it with multiple compilers. Three of the more popular tools, Zinc (by Zinc Software), zApp (by Inmark Development), and XVT (by XVT Software), are also available for multiple platforms; they can generate code for DOS text and graphics modes, Windows, and even Unix. All of this is possible while maintaining compatibility with several compilers. These three tools are specific to C++ programmers, but similar tools are available for other languages.

Language and Platform Compatibility

Many of the tools mentioned in this chapter are available on multiple development platforms. There are several key items to remember when picking tools.

First, choose a language that you like, and that you understand. This cannot be underestimated; without a firm understanding—and yes, even a great fondness—of your programming language, you will not be as proficient as you could be.

Second, look for an environment (for your selected language) from a company that has good support from third-party vendors. Third party support means that libraries of code, example programs, books, and articles will be available for your programming environment. These tools will speed up your development time and your learning curve, and should not be overlooked. Look in any of the popular programming magazines, especially at the advertisements for program libraries; look specifically at the compiler environments that are listed. If the environment you are considering is not there, call a few of the vendors, and ask if support is available. Sometimes only the most popular compiler environments will be listed in the ads.

Be sure to find out whether the compiler you want to use is supported by the debugger, source control, and design tools that interest you. Perhaps some of these tools will be built into the compiler's environment. If not, can they be well integrated? Don't be afraid to call the third-party vendors and ask how well their tools work with specific compilers.

Third, look for a compiler that is available for your chosen programming environment. Some compilers only support one environment: DOS, Windows, OS/2, Unix, Motif, or Vax/VMS for instance. Others will support multiple platforms.

There are two parts to the environment question. Does the compiler (and its related tools) run in the environment, and does the compiler create programs that run in the environment? For instance, there are compilers that run under Windows, but that only create DOS programs; there are also DOS compilers that create Windows programs.

Once you adopt an environment, you will want your compiler and tools to run there. If they don't, you will waste a lot of valuable time switching from one environment to another to use the tools. Plan in advance, and look for the tools that directly support your chosen environment.

What Next?

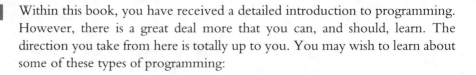

Within this book, you have received a detailed introduction to programming. However, there is a great deal more that you can, and should, learn. The direction you take from here is totally up to you. You may wish to learn about some of these types of programming:

- ◆ C and C++ programming
- ◆ Pascal programming
- ◆ Object-oriented programming
- ◆ Event-driven programming
- ◆ Programming with GUIs
- ◆ Mathematical programming with FORTRAN
- ◆ Visual GUI programming with Visual Basic
- ◆ Visual GUI programming with C++
- ◆ Programming for Unix
- ◆ Business programming with COBOL

Start with one area that interests you, and branch out as you feel the need, or as requirements arise. Appendix D lists some books and magazines that will help you continue in your quest to become a programmer.

Above all, remember that the best way to learn and grow in this endeavor is to keep programming.

Thus spake the master programmer:

"After three days without programming, life becomes meaningless."

—The Tao of Programming

Appendix A

ASCII and EBCDIC Characters,

and Their Corresponding

Numeric Values

THIS Appendix consists largely of the table below, which serves two purposes. First, it shows the correlations between numbers in different numbering systems. Second, it shows the characters available in the ASCII (American Standard Code for Information Interchange) and EBCDIC (Extended Binary Coded Decimal Information Code) character sets.

remember: *In ASCII, the characters numbered 1 through 127 are known as the standard characters; they are available on all ASCII-based computers. The extended characters, numbered 128 through 255, are less commonly used; these characters are available only on IBM-compatible personal computers.*

Decimal Number	Binary Number	Octal Number	Hex Number	ASCII Character	EBCDIC Character
0	00000000	000	00		NUL
1	00000001	001	01	☺	SOH
2	00000010	002	02	☻	STX
3	00000011	003	03	♥	ETX
4	00000100	004	04	♦	PF
5	00000101	005	05	♣	HT
6	00000110	006	06	♠	LC
7	00000111	007	07	•	DEL
8	00001000	010	08	◘	
9	00001001	011	09	○	RLF
10	00001010	012	0A	◙	SMM
11	00001011	013	0B	♂	VT
12	00001100	014	0C	♀	FF
13	00001101	015	0D	♪	CR
14	00001110	016	0E	♫	RES

ASCII AND EBCDIC CHARACTERS, AND THEIR CORRESPONDING NUMERIC VALUES

Decimal Number	Binary Number	Octal Number	Hex Number	ASCII Character	EBCDIC Character
15	00001111	017	0F	✿	SI
16	00010000	020	10	►	DLE
17	00010001	021	11	◄	DC1
18	00010010	022	12	↕	DC2
19	00010011	023	13	‼	DC3
20	00010100	024	14	¶	
21	00010101	025	15	§	NL
22	00010110	026	16	■	BS
23	00010111	027	17	↨	IL
24	00011000	030	18	↑	CAN
25	00011001	031	19	↓	EM
26	00011010	032	1A	→	CC
27	00011011	033	1B	←	
28	00011100	034	1C	∟	IFS
29	00011101	035	1D	↔	
30	00011110	036	1E	▲	IRS
31	00011111	037	1F	▼	IUS
32	00100000	040	20	(space)	DS
33	00100001	041	21	!	SOS
34	00100010	042	22	"	FS
35	00100011	043	23	#	
36	00100100	044	24	$	BYP
37	00100101	045	25	%	LF
38	00100110	046	26	&	EOB
39	00100111	047	27	'	ESC
40	00101000	050	28	(	
41	00101001	051	29	)	
42	00101010	052	2A	*	SM
43	00101011	053	2B	+	
44	00101100	054	2C	,	
45	00101101	055	2D	–	ENQ
46	00101110	056	2E	.	ACK
47	00101111	057	2F	/	BEL
48	00110000	060	30	0	
49	00110001	061	31	1	
50	00110010	062	32	2	SYN
51	00110011	063	33	3	
52	00110100	064	34	4	PN
53	00110101	065	35	5	RS
54	00110110	066	36	6	UC
55	00110111	067	37	7	EOT
56	00111000	070	38	8	

Decimal Number	Binary Number	Octal Number	Hex Number	ASCII Character	EBCDIC Character
57	00111001	071	39	9	
58	00111010	072	3A	:	
59	00111011	073	3B	;	
60	00111100	074	3C	<	DC4
61	00111101	075	3D	=	NAK
62	00111110	076	3E	>	
63	00111111	077	3F	?	SUB
64	01000000	100	40	@	(space)
65	01000001	101	41	A	
66	01000010	102	42	B	
67	01000011	103	43	C	
68	01000100	104	44	D	
69	01000101	105	45	E	
70	01000110	106	46	F	
71	01000111	107	47	G	
72	01001000	110	48	H	
73	01001001	111	49	I	
74	01001010	112	4A	J	¢
75	01001011	113	4B	K	.
76	01001100	114	4C	L	<
77	01001101	115	4D	M	(
78	01001110	116	4E	N	+
79	01001111	117	4F	O	
80	01010000	120	50	P	&
81	01010001	121	51	Q	
82	01010010	122	52	R	
83	01010011	123	53	S	
84	01010100	124	54	T	
85	01010101	125	55	U	
86	01010110	126	56	V	
87	01010111	127	57	W	
88	01011000	130	58	X	
89	01011001	131	59	Y	
90	01011010	132	5A	Z	!
91	01011011	133	5B	[	$
92	01011100	134	5C	\	*
93	01011101	135	5D	]	)
94	01011110	136	5E	^	;
95	01011111	137	5F	_	¬
96	01100000	140	60	`	-
97	01100001	141	61	a	/
98	01100010	142	62	b	

Decimal Number	Binary Number	Octal Number	Hex Number	ASCII Character	EBCDIC Character
99	01100011	143	63	c	
100	01100100	144	64	d	
101	01100101	145	65	e	
102	01100110	146	66	f	
103	01100111	147	67	g	
104	01101000	150	68	h	
105	01101001	151	69	i	
106	01101010	152	6A	j		
107	01101011	153	6B	k	,
108	01101100	154	6C	l	%
109	01101101	155	6D	m	_
110	01101110	156	6E	n	>
111	01101111	157	6F	o	?
112	01110000	160	70	p	
113	01110001	161	71	q	
114	01110010	162	72	r	
115	01110011	163	73	s	
116	01110100	164	74	t	
117	01110101	165	75	u	
118	01110110	166	76	v	
119	01110111	167	77	w	
120	01111000	170	78	x	
121	01111001	171	79	y	
122	01111010	172	7A	z	:
123	01111011	173	7B	{	#
124	01111100	174	7C	|	@
125	01111101	175	7D	}	'
126	01111110	176	7E	~	=
127	01111111	177	7F	⌂	"
128	10000000	200	80	Ç	
129	10000001	201	81	ü	a
130	10000010	202	82	é	b
131	10000011	203	83	â	c
132	10000100	204	84	ä	d
133	10000101	205	85	à	e
134	10000110	206	86	å	f
135	10000111	207	87	ç	g
136	10001000	210	88	ê	h
137	10001001	211	89	ë	i
138	10001010	212	8A	è	
139	10001011	213	8B	ï	
140	10001100	214	8C	î	

Decimal Number	Binary Number	Octal Number	Hex Number	ASCII Character	EBCDIC Character
141	10001101	215	8D	ì	
142	10001110	216	8E	Ä	
143	10001111	217	8F	Å	
144	10010000	220	90	É	
145	10010001	221	91	æ	j
146	10010010	222	92	Æ	k
147	10010011	223	93	ô	l
148	10010100	224	94	ö	m
149	10010101	225	95	ò	n
150	10010110	226	96	û	o
151	10010111	227	97	ù	p
152	10011000	230	98	ÿ	q
153	10011001	231	99	Ö	r
154	10011010	232	9A	Ü	
155	10011011	233	9B	¢	
156	10011100	234	9C	£	
157	10011101	235	9D	¥	
158	10011110	236	9E	Pt	
159	10011111	237	9F	ƒ	
160	10100000	240	A0	á	
161	10100001	241	A1	í	~
162	10100010	242	A2	ó	s
163	10100011	243	A3	ú	t
164	10100100	244	A4	ñ	u
165	10100101	245	A5	Ñ	v
166	10100110	246	A6	ª	w
167	10100111	247	A7	º	x
168	10101000	250	A8	¿	y
169	10101001	251	A9	⌐	z
170	10101010	252	AA	¬	
171	10101011	253	AB	½	
172	10101100	254	AC	¼	
173	10101101	255	AD	¡	
174	10101110	256	AE	«	
175	10101111	257	AF	»	
176	10110000	260	B0	▓	
177	10110001	261	B1	█	
178	10110010	262	B2	█	
179	10110011	263	B3	│	
180	10110100	264	B4	┤	
181	10110101	265	B5	╡	
182	10110110	266	B6	╢	

Decimal Number	Binary Number	Octal Number	Hex Number	ASCII Character	EBCDIC Character
183	10110111	267	B7	ฦ	
184	10111000	270	B8	ฃ	
185	10111001	271	B9	ฟ	
186	10111010	272	BA	‖	
187	10111011	273	BB	ฦ	
188	10111100	274	BC	ฦ	
189	10111101	275	BD	ฦ	
190	10111110	276	BE	ฃ	
191	10111111	277	BF	ฃ	
192	11000000	300	C0	ฃ	{
193	11000001	301	C1	ฃ	A
194	11000010	302	C2	ฅ	B
195	11000011	303	C3	ฃ	C
196	11000100	304	C4	—	D
197	11000101	305	C5	ฃ	E
198	11000110	306	C6	ฃ	F
199	11000111	307	C7	ฃ	G
200	11001000	310	C8	ฃ	H
201	11001001	311	C9	ฃ	I
202	11001010	312	CA	ฃ	
203	11001011	313	CB	ฃ	
204	11001100	314	CC	ฃ	
205	11001101	315	CD	–	
206	11001110	316	CE	ฃ	
207	11001111	317	CF	ฃ	
208	11010000	320	D0	ฃ	}
209	11010001	321	D1	ฃ	J
210	11010010	322	D2	ฃ	K
211	11010011	323	D3	ฃ	L
212	11010100	324	D4	ฃ	M
213	11010101	325	D5	ฃ	N
214	11010110	326	D6	ฃ	O
215	11010111	327	D7	ฃ	P
216	11011000	330	D8	ฃ	Q
217	11011001	331	D9	ฃ	R
218	11011010	332	DA	ฃ	
219	11011011	333	DB	▮	
220	11011100	334	DC	▪	
221	11011101	335	DD	▌	
222	11011110	336	DE	▐	
223	11011111	337	DF	▪	
224	11100000	340	E0	α	

Decimal Number	Binary Number	Octal Number	Hex Number	ASCII Character	EBCDIC Character
225	11100001	341	E1	β	
226	11100010	342	E2	Γ	S
227	11100011	343	E3	π	T
228	11100100	344	E4	Σ	U
229	11100101	345	E5	σ	V
230	11100110	346	E6	μ	W
231	11100111	347	E7	τ	X
232	11101000	350	E8	φ	Y
233	11101001	351	E9	θ	Z
234	11101010	352	EA	Ω	
235	11101011	353	EB	δ	
236	11101100	354	EC	∞	
237	11101101	355	ED	∅	
238	11101110	356	EE	∈	
239	11101111	357	EF	∩	
240	11110000	360	F0	≡	0
241	11110001	361	F1	±	1
242	11110010	362	F2	≥	2
243	11110011	363	F3	≤	3
244	11110100	364	F4	⌠	4
245	11110101	365	F5	⌡	5
246	11110110	366	F6	÷	6
247	11110111	367	F7	≈	7
248	11111000	370	F8	°	8
249	11111001	371	F9	•	9
250	11111010	372	FA	•	
251	11111011	373	FB	√	
252	11111100	374	FC	η_2	
253	11111101	375	FD		
254	11111110	376	FE	■	
255	11111111	377	FF		

Notice that in the table above, the EBCDIC column shows a number of two-character and three-character mnemonics. Most EBCDIC computers will not display these values; they are used in data communications, to perform special functions. The use of these mnemonics allows a command to be transmitted in a single byte.

Some of the more common mnemonics are listed in the table shown next, each with a description of its use. As with the character sets, the ASCII and EBCDIC standards use different values for these special commands. The EBCDIC values for these commands are shown in the preceding table; you will notice in this table that there are already display characters listed for the extended ASCII values. This is because the ASCII standard allows each of these special commands to be displayed as a single character on a computer screen. The ASCII values that correspond to these mnemonics are shown in the following table:

ASCII Value	Mnemonic Transmission Code	Meaning
0	NUL	Null, or zero, value
2	STX	Beginning of text
3	ETX	End of text
5	ENQ	Enquire
6	ACK	Acknowledge
7	BEL	Bell
8	BS	Backspace
9	HT	Horizontal tab
10	LF	Line feed
11	VT	Vertical tab
12	FF	Form feed
13	CR	Carriage return
21	NAK	Negative acknowledge
24	CAN	Cancel
27	ESC	Escape
127	DEL	Delete

Appendix B

A Programming Glossary

T H I S appendix describes much of the lingo you will hear as a programmer, but it is more than just a reference. There are a number of terms described here that do not appear earlier in the book; nonetheless, it is important that you, as a programmer, familiarize yourself with these terms.

ADA

A language developed under the direction of the United States Department of Defense. ADA is now required on many government projects. Like Pascal, it is a very large language (meaning that it requires a great deal of disk space and computational power to execute), but it offers an extensive list of features and capabilities.

Address

A specific memory location within the computer.

Alpha test

The first phase of testing on a computer program. Alpha testing is usually done by the programmer, or within the programmer's company, before any end-users are allowed to use the product. This testing precedes the beta test.

Analog signal

A type of signal used for transmitting sound. This is a signal that is not easily quantifiable; an analog signal can have any continuous value, as opposed to a digital signal, in which specific, measurable values will be present. *See also* Digital signal.

ANSI

American National Standards Institute. ANSI is an organization that approves standards for computer languages (among many other things). For instance, ANSI C is now the standard to which all C compiler vendors must comply.

Following this type of standard allows for better movement of your code from one compiler or platform to another.

Append

Add to the end. This term is used most often with file processing; appending information to a file implies adding it to the end of the file.

Argument

See Parameter.

Array

A group of like items which are referred to with a numeric index. An array of ten integers, for instance, contains similar items (all integers), but they can have different values. Each element in the array is referred to as array[1], array[2], etc.

Artificial intelligence (AI)

The study of how to make computers act more like human beings. The original test for an AI program was performed as follows: A person would sit in a room with several computer terminals. Upon each one, a series of questions and answers would be typed. If the person could not tell whether they were conversing with a computer or a human on the other end, the program being run was thought to have some degree of artificial intelligence. One common application which has resulted from AI research is expert systems.

ASCII

American Standard Code for Information Interchange. A standard definition for how each byte of information is interpreted (e.g., as a letter, number, special character, etc.).

ASCII file

A file that only contains ASCII characters (with no extra codes to indicate formatting, font selection, etc.). Batch files and source code files are examples of ASCII files. Also known as "straight ASCII files." *See also* Binary file.

Assembler

A program that converts Assembly Language statements into machine language for use by the computer.

Assignment

The process of giving a new value to a variable.

BASIC

Beginner's All-purpose Symbolic Instruction Code. A programming language that is included on almost evey PC sold, and which is simpler to learn than many languages.

Batch file

A file that contains commands to be given to the operating system.

BBS

See Bulletin board system.

BCPL

A language that was the precursor for the C language. It is no longer in common use.

Beta test

The second round of testing on a computer program. A beta test generally involves using several regular or potential customers to test the program. This is usually the last stage of testing in which any major changes can be made.

Binary

A numbering system in which the numbers can only have two values: 0 and 1. Binary is the numbering system used internally by computers, since they only handle on(1) and off(0) positions within their electronic minds.

Binary file

A file that can contain any sequence of bytes, whether or not they can be read by humans. Executable (program) files, object files, and library files are all examples of binary files. *See also* ASCII file.

Binary search

A search technique used with items that are in a sorted order. You first look at the middle item in a list, thereby eliminating the top half of the list for the next round of the search. In each subsequent round, searching begins with the middle item of the remaining half, effectively cutting the search area in half with each check.

BIOS

Basic Input and Output System. The code built into each computer to handle the movement of data from the peripheral input and output devices to the central processor.

Bit

Binary digIT. The smallest item of storage within a computer, a bit can only hold the value 0 or 1.

Boolean

A type of variable that holds a value of either TRUE or FALSE.

Bottom-up

A design technique which involves designing the specific functions that need to be performed first, and then trying to tie the functions together into subprograms and programs. *See also* Top-down.

Breakpoint

A place marked in your source code where the program will stop, so that you can look at what is happening, what values each variable has, etc. Used in debugging your programs.

Bubble sort

A sort technique that involves moving small values to the top of a list until the entire list is sorted. A bubble sort is simple to implement, but there are more efficient techniques available if you need speed.

Bug

Something that is in your program that causes it to act in an unexpected manner.

Bulletin board system

A computer that is set up to receive calls from other computers, allowing the transfer and sharing of files, messages, and other information.

Button

A small area on the computer screen that looks and acts like a standard push-button. Buttons provide program users with a graphical means of selecting options or activating program functions.

Byte

A unit of eight bits of information. A byte is the smallest piece of memory dealt with by most programs. A byte can hold one ASCII character, or one number in the range 0 through 255.

C

A language that is commonly used for systems-level programming, where great control of the computer is required.

C++

An updated version of the C language that includes object-oriented programming capabilities.

■■■■■
Calling program

A program that starts the execution of a function, subroutine, or procedure.

■■■■■
CASE

See Computer-aided software engineering.

■■■■■
CASE statement

A statement that allows a specific piece of the program to execute based upon the value of a specific variable.

■■■■■
CGA

Color Graphics Adapter. A low-resolution graphics adapter common on early PCs. Typical resolution for CGA graphics was 320×200 pixels.

■■■■■
Class

The definition of an object in C++, and many other object-oriented programming languages.

■■■■■
Client

A computer program that is the recipient of information from a server. Requests for information are sent to the server by the client, usually through a computer network. The server acts upon the requests, and returns the correct information, also through the network.

■■■■■
COBOL

COmmon Business Oriented Language. A language designed for use in business and financial programming.

■■■■■
Code

The part of a computer program that contains statements specifying what the program is to do.

Comment

A statement in your program that helps to document what the program is for or how the variables are used. Comments do not affect a program's execution.

Compiler

A computer program that converts source code, written in a programming language, into machine code, which can then be executed by the computer.

Computer-aided software engineering (CASE)

A process by which a computer is used in the software development process to guide the design and possibly even generate some of the required source code.

Conditional statements

Statements that allow a program to follow one of several paths, based on a condition that must be met or a decision that needs to be made.

Constant

A value in a program that cannot change during the program's execution. *See also* Variable.

Context-sensitive help

Helpful or instructional text that is related to the activity currently being performed by the program user, and that is designed by the programmer to appear onscreen at the user's request.

CPU

Central Processing Unit. The CPU is the brain of the computer, in which all calculations and decisions take place.

CRT

Cathode Ray Tube. Historical name for terminals that were connected to mainframes and minicomputers. Now, it is often used to refer to monitors on PCs.

Cursor

The blinking pointer on the computer screen that shows where your next keystrokes will appear.

Data

The information that is used and stored by programs.

Data entry

The process of entering information into a program.

Data processing

The process of taking raw data and using it to produce meaningful information.

Database management system (DBMS)

A program whose specific task is to manage information stored in one or more files on a disk drive. This includes adding, updating, and deleting information to these files, as well as creating and destroying the data files themselves.

Debug

To find and eliminate bugs from a computer program.

Decrement

To reduce a numeric value, usually by 1.

Desk check

A test that is performed by the programmer, usually alone or at his or her own desk, before a program is released for alpha and beta testing. This test checks the program for correct operations. Once the the desk check is successfully completed, the program is tested again with programs written by other programmers on the team.

DFD

Data Flow Diagram. A type of drawing used to depict the various processes in a computer program and the flow of data between those processes.

Dialog box

A special type of window in which the program effectively has a dialog with the user, asking for information that is required for the program to continue.

Digital signal

A type of signal used for transmitting sound. A digital signal uses specific, measurable values to represent information. *See also* Analog signal.

Disassembler

A program that attempts to generate source code from machine language code. A disassembler is often used to determine how a program is written, and is useful when the original programmer is no longer available, or when the original source code has been misplaced.

DOS

Disk Operating System. DOS is the software that resides on your computer and handles communications between your programs and the computer itself. Two common flavors of DOS are MS-DOS from Microsoft, and PC-DOS from IBM.

Download

To receive information, data, or files on one computer that have been transmitted from another computer.

DP department

In a corporate environment, a department that performs data processing functions.

DPMI

DOS Protected–Mode Interface is a method for controlling how programs will act in memory while operating in *protected mode*. *See also* Protected mode.

Dynamic memory allocation

The reservation of a certain amount of memory outside the program itself, for use during a program's execution.

E-mail

Electronic mail. The process of sending and receiving messages by electronic means, such as online services and bulletin boards.

Editor

A program used for creating and refining computer programs. There are two basic types of editors: full-screen editors and line editors. Full-screen editors let you move easily to different locations in your files and on the computer screen. Line editors, on the other hand, only let you edit a single line of code at a time.

EGA

Extended Graphics Adapter. The second generation of graphics adapters (a refinement over the earlier CGA adapters), EGA can support a resolution of 640×350 pixels.

Element

One member, or item, in an array.

Encapsulation

The process of combining data and processing capabilities within an object, and then concealing them from outside view.

End-user

The person who will finally use a computer program.

Event-driven

A system of programming in which applications must react to various external events, rather than following a straight, immutable path.

Expert system

A program that maintains a body of rules and knowledge, attempting to replicate the knowledge of an expert in a specific field.

Extension

The three letters that follow the period in a filename on DOS-based computers.

FHD

Function Hierarchy Diagram. A type of drawing that shows the relationship between the primary functions in a computer program and the smaller functions that are used to complete them.

Field

In a database program, a single piece of data, such as a name or a phone number. *See also* Record.

File

A named section on a computer's disk drive that maintains an established collection of information, usually relating to a specific topic.

File handle

A number that is used by a computer program to refer to a specific file. A file handle is assigned when the file is opened.

float

A variable in C and C++ used for floating-point, or real, numbers.

Flow chart

A drawing that shows how a computer program (or in fact, any activity) will function on a step-by-step basis.

FORTRAN

FORmula TRANslation language, originally developed for use in number-intensive programming.

Fourth-generation language (4GL)

A language designed to provide the end-user with a simple means of writing programs. Typical 4GL languages are used to enhance or streamline the use of database management systems.

Free-form language

A type of language in which the source code requires no specific formatting. Generally, FORTRAN and RPG are not free-form languages, while C, C++, Pascal, and BASIC are.

Full-screen editor

See Editor.

Function

A named section of a program that performs a specific task. In most languages (other than C/C++), a function returns a value to the main, or calling, program.

Gamma test

Usually the last test before software is released to end-users. The gamma test is the final shake-out, and not many changes are usually allowed during this phase of testing. Not all companies perform gamma tests; some simply release their product after a successful beta test.

GIGO

Garbage In, Garbage Out. The idea that whatever level of programs and data you put into your computer are the same level that you will be able to retrieve. "If you put good stuff in, you get good stuff out"; the reverse is also true.

Global variable

A variable that may be accessed from any function, procedure, or subroutine throughout the entire program.

Graphics adapter

A special card, resident inside the computer, that deals with the display of graphical images on the monitor.

GUI

Graphical User Interface. The display for a program that uses pictures and graphical elements to convey information to the user.

Hard copy

The printed version of a report or diagram. Hard copy exists on paper.

Hardware

The computing machinery needed to process your program. Hardware includes the computer itself and all peripheral devices, such as the modem and printer.

Header file

In C and C++, a special file used to maintain definitions of certain data types and processes that are available for use in every program you create.

Hex

Short for Hexadecimal. The base-16 numbering system, which uses the numbers 0 through 9 and the letters A through F to represent 16 possible digits.

High-level language

A language that is closer to English than to machine language. Such languages include C, C++, BASIC, Pascal, FORTRAN, COBOL, and many others.

I/O

Input and Output. The movement of data from the computer's peripheral devices to the central processor.

IC (Integrated circuit)

A chip inside the computer. This includes the processor (8088, 80286, 80386, 80486, Pentium, 68000, 68020, etc.), as well as the math coprocessor, memory chips, and input/output chips.

Increment

To increase the value of a number, usually by one.

Index

1. In structured programming, the variable used in a loop to track the number of times the loop has run.

2. In arrays, the number used to specify a certain entry in the array (for example, the index 1 refers to the first item in a Pascal array).

Infinite loop

A loop, or section of code, that continues to run forever.

Inheritance

In object-oriented programming, the ability to create new objects that take certain attributes from their parent objects. This process is similar to inheritance in people: Children inherit many of their parents' attributes, and then develop some of their own.

Input

The process of getting information into a program.

Integer

A whole number.

Interface

The method in which a program or computer can talk to another program, computer, or device.

Interpreter

A program that reads and executes source code written in a programming language.

ISAM

Indexed Sequential Access Method. ISAM is a technique, popular on mainframe computers, for quickly locating information in a data file.

JCL

Job Control Language. Similar in concept to batch file programming, but used on mainframe computers and some minicomputers.

K (kilobytes)

A unit of 1024 bytes. Generally used for discussing memory or disk drive space on a computer.

Keyboard

The standard data entry device for a computer; it looks much like a typewriter, with approximately 80 to 100 separate keys, each representing an individual character.

Keyword

A special word that can only have a single, specific use in a given computer language. For instance, most languages will not allow you to name a variable **IF**, because **IF** is a keyword that already has a special meaning in the language.

LAN

Local Area Network. A cluster of computers, all connected to each other in such a way that allows sharing of data and messages. Generally, a single LAN will reside in one department or building. *See also* WAN.

Library

A set of functions that have been compiled and debugged, and that are stored together for use in other programs.

Line editor

See Editor.

Local variable

A variable that can only be used and referenced within a single subroutine, function, or procedure.

Logical

See Boolean.

Look and feel

The appearance and functioning of a program from the user's perspective. The look and feel includes the types of menus, the required keypresses, colors, screen layouts, etc. The purpose of graphical user interfaces is to present a common, familiar look and feel for many programs; this allows for simpler training across multiple programs.

Loop

In structured programming, a tool that allows one or more lines of code to be repeated a given number of times, or until a specific condition is met.

Low-level language

A language that is closer to the language the computer understands than to English. Assembly language and machine language are generally thought of as low-level languages.

Machine language

The language that the computer understands. Machine language generally resembles a sequence of numbers, and is very difficult for humans to read and follow.

Macro language

A small programming language that is built into an application, allowing the user to customize the application, or to repeat a series of functions using minimal time and effort.

Mainframe

A larger computer, usually characterized by dozens (or hundreds) of users on separate terminals (CRTs).

Man-year

See People-year.

Meg

Short for megabyte. A meg is the same as 1000 K, or 1,024,000 bytes.

Member function

See Method.

Menu

A set of possible choices, each representing a function that can be performed by a program. The choice made by the user will determine which function is performed.

Method

In object-oriented programming, a procedure within a class that determines how the class will operate.

Methodology

A set of standards to be followed during a process. For instance, a software development methodology might specify the types of diagrams to be used during the design of a program, the order in which the diagrams should be produced, etc.

Microcomputer

A small, single-user computer.

Microprocessor

The CPU within a microcomputer.

Minicomputer

A midsized computer that can have anywhere from one to a few dozen users.

MIS department

Management Information Services. In a corporate environment, the group that works with raw data on the computers to determine and generate the information that management will need for running the business.

Mnemonic

A short name, or an abbreviation. *See also* TLA.

Modem

MOdulator-DEModulator. A computer peripheral that converts computer information (which is digital) into an *analog signal* that can be transmitted across a telephone line, and then converts any information received from analog back to digital. Modems are used to allow for communication between computers, online services, and bulletin boards.

Modula-2

A computer language, based on Pascal, that was designed specifically to handle large projects.

Monitor

The video component of a computer, upon which most output is presented.

Monochrome

Having multiple shades of one color, rather than multiple colors. Used to describe video display and hard copy.

Motif

A GUI that is common on Unix systems.

Multiprocessor

A computer that uses more than one CPU to perform its calculation and processing functions.

Multitasking

Processing several different tasks at the same time. Generally, multitasking is done on a computer by dividing the CPU's time among the tasks so that they take turns accessing the CPU.

Multimedia

A recently developed approach to presenting information through several types of media, including video, sound, and motion.

Nesting

Including one thing inside another. A loop that runs within another loop is considered to be nested within the outer loop. If a comment appears within another comment, the inside comment is called a *nested* comment.

Network

See LAN.

Non-volatile

Not destined to be lost when the computer is turned off. For instance, hard disk storage is non-volatile, because it remains available between each use of the computer. By contrast, information stored in the computer's memory is volatile, because it is erased each time the computer is turned off.

Null string

A string with nothing in it, with a length of zero.

Oberon

A simplified, object-oriented descendent of the Modula-2 programming language.

Object-oriented programming (OOP)

A programming style in which the programmer focuses on developing self-contained objects, instead of on a broad, overall plan for the program.

Off-site

A storage location that is away from the program development site. Very often, development teams will store a copy of their source code in a separate location in case of fire or other catastrophe.

Online services

Electronic, computer-based services that can be accessed by a computer with a modem. These include such services as CompuServe, Prodigy, and America Online.

OOP

See Object-oriented programming.

Operating system

The computer program that is responsible for managing the resources of the computer, the starting and ending of programs, etc.

Operators

1. People who run programs. *See* End-users.

2. Special characters used to perform an operation on one or more numbers, such as +, −, *, etc.

Optimization

Making a computer program, or portions of a program, run faster or with fewer computer resources (less memory, disk space, etc.).

PAL

Paradox Application Language, a programming language used with the Paradox database management system by Borland.

Paradigm shift

A change in a previously established way of thinking.

Parallel arrays

Multiple arrays, each with the same number of elements, in which an item in one array is related to the item having the same index in another array.

Parallel test

A test performed with the end-user, in which an old system and new system are both run for a period of time to verify that the new system is producing the same (or the desired) results.

Parameter

A piece of data that is passed into a function, procedure, or subroutine.

Pascal

A programming language well-suited for teaching structured programming.

PC

Personal Computer, or microcomputer.

People-year

The amount of programming work that can be completed by one person in one year of full-time work.

Peripherals

Hardware devices that are connected to a computer, such as printers, keyboards, monitors, modems, etc.

Pixel

From Picture (pix) Element (el). A single dot on a computer screen. The dots are used to create characters that are read on the screen, as well as graphical images which can be viewed.

Polymorphism

The capacity for multiple items to have the same name. For example, polymorphism allows a single name to be used for several procedures that all perform a similar function, but that use different parameter types. The programmer then does not have to remember different names for each of the procedures.

Portability

The ability of a computer program to be used on many computer platforms, and with numerous compilers, without any revision. Complete portability is not generally possible, but by using it as a goal, programmers can create applications that require minimal changes from platform to platform.

Private

In object-oriented programming, refers to methods and data within an object or class that cannot be viewed outside of that object.

Procedural language

A language that is used to write procedural programs (as opposed to object-oriented programs), in which the sequence of events is wholly controlled by the programmer.

Procedural problems

Problems related to the procedures embodied in a program or system—that is, how the program or system is actually used. *See also* Systematic problems.

Procedure

A named piece of code that performs a specific task. In most languages, a procedure will not return a value to the calling program.

Profiler

A program that monitors the execution of your programs, and determines where most of the programming time is spent. Helpful when you are trying to optimize your programs for speed.

Program

A sequence of commands, written in a computer language, that control what the computer is to do.

Program generator

A specialized computer program that is used for generating standard source code to perform a limited set of functions.

Programmer

A person who writes computer programs. Various types of programmers and levels of programming exist.

Prolog

A language used in the artificial intelligence community, especially in the area of expert systems design. It is structured very much like the IF...THEN rules that are common in expert systems, and therefore provides an understandable method of incorporating rules in a program.

Protected

In object-oriented programming, refers to methods and data within an object or class that cannot be viewed outside of that object, except by other objects of the same type, or by inherited types.

Protected mode

A special processing mode available on PCs that allows access to the entire range of available memory, rather than just the 640K available to DOS programs.

Prototype

A small program that is used to show the conceptual use of a new program. It allows the look and feel of the program to be designed without requiring that the main portion of the code be written.

Pseudocode

A structured English representation of a section of code. Usually, pseudocode bears great resemblance to the language that will be used in the final coding.

Public

In object-oriented programming, refers to methods and data within an object or class that can be viewed outside of that object.

Pull-down menu

A vertical menu, with a moving selection bar, that looks like it has been pulled down from another menu (the way a shade is pulled down over a window).

RAM

Random Access Memory. Memory that can be used, written, and read by any program.

Real

A designation for a floating point number.

Record

One line of a data file, in which all the information about one item in the file is kept. For instance, in an address book, each record deals with one person in the book. Each item within the record (name, address, phone, etc.) is considered a field.

REM

Short for REMark, REM is used to denote a comment, or remark, in a BASIC program.

Resolution

Refers to the number of dots, or pixels, on a computer screen; the more pixels there are, the higher the resolution (and the sharper the screen image) will be. Also, the accuracy of numbers as they get smaller and smaller.

Robust

The ability of a program to handle unknown or unexpected events. The better the computer can respond, the more robust it is considered.

ROM

Read Only Memory. An area of memory on the computer in which the contents can never change. Generally, ROM is used to store the computer's BIOS (Basic Input and Output System), since there are no changes required to this program.

RPG

RePort Generation language. A language that is used in business applications to generate reports from raw data organized in files.

Screen generator

A specialized computer program that is used for drawing (or creating) computer screen layouts, and for then generating standard source code to perform a limited set of functions with those screens.

Self-modifying code

A program that can modify itself. Using self-modifying code is a wonderful way to burn out a programmer who is responsible for debugging or maintenance, because it is nearly impossible to follow code that changes while it is running.

Sequential search

A search method that starts at the beginning of a list, and looks at each element until it finds the item being searched for.

Server

A computer program that handles requests for information or processing from client programs. Requests for information are sent to the server by the client, usually through a computer network. The server acts upon the requests, and returns the correct information, also through the network.

Site license

A special license for software that allows a company to use as many copies of the software as desired, within a single site, at a single cost.

Software

The programs, or instructions, that make a computer work.

Software license

An agreement that allows an end-user to use a piece of software. The ownership of the software remains with the developer.

Sort

The process of putting a list or series of items in some order, usually numerical or alphabetical.

Source code

The original language of a program, written in a programming language such as C, BASIC, or Pascal.

Spaghetti code

Poorly structured code that is difficult to follow and understand. Very often, such needless complexity results from the excessive use of **GOTO** statements.

SQL

Structured Query Language, or Sequel, a language that is common for use in database management systems.

Standards manual

A book or report that states the programming rules that will be followed in a company or department.

Statements

The specific lines of code or commands in a program.

Static memory

The reservation of memory within a program, determined prior to compilation of the program, for use during a program's execution.

String

A sequence of characters, such as a word or a sentence.

Structured programming

A type of programming in which the tasks that are to be performed are broken down into separate functions and subroutines. In structured programming, the use of **GOTO** statements is reduced or eliminated through the use of looping and conditional statements.

Structured walkthrough

A special type of testing, usually performed with a group of programmers working on the same project, in which the code is checked, one line at a time, for consistency and correct execution.

Subroutine

A named piece of code that performs a specific task. In most languages, subroutines have the option of returning a value to the calling program.

Supercomputers

Large computers, which may have one or many users, and which are usually dedicated to calculation-intensive tasks, such as cryptography and real-time generation of high-resolution graphic images.

Syntax

The words and structures used in a computer language.

Syntax error

An error in a program that is caused by misuse of a word or structure.

Systematic problems

Problems related to the actual computer hardware and software (programs) used in a system. These can involve program bugs, as well as the use of software that was not designed with the correct purposes in mind. *See also* Procedural problems.

Systems analysis

The process of defining the problems that exist in a computer system, and determining the best methods of solving the problems, whether they be systematic or procedural.

Terminator

The character used to end a string. In many languages, including C and C++, the terminator is the null character (which appears as a blank space, and has an ASCII value of 0).

TLA

Three Letter Acronym. You may notice the number of TLAs in this appendix; they seem to be very common in the computing industry.

Top-down

An approach to software design that starts at the top, defining the goal of the program, and then breaking each needed function down to lower levels, until each subfunction can be assigned to a specific program subroutine. *See also* Bottom-up.

TUI

Text-based User Interface. A standardized interface that, unlike a GUI, does not make use of graphical images. This makes a TUI less attractive, but TUIs are known to be much faster than GUIs!

Unix

A popular multitasking, multiuser operating system that was written in C.

Upload

To send information, data, or files from one computer to another.

Upward compatibility

The ability of a program to use the files generated by earlier versions of the same program. If the data can move to higher revision numbers (from version 1.0 to version 2.0, for instance), then the files are said to be upwardly compatible.

User

The person who finally runs a program. *See also* End–user.

User interface

The part of a program that the user can see.

User-friendly

Refers to a program that has been written with the user in mind, so that the interface is designed to be simple and intuitive.

Utility

A specialized program written to perform a specific function.

Validity check

A verification performed on a field, or another unit of information, to match it against certain criteria. For example, a number may need to fall within a given range, a string may need to be shorter than a certain length, etc.

Variable

A location in memory that is used to store data.

VGA

Video Graphics Array. The third generation of graphics adapters, representing a refinement over the earlier EGA adapters. A standard that provides graphic resolution of 640×480 pixels.

vi

A programmer's text editor, popular with designers of Unix systems.

Visual Basic

A compiler for writing Microsoft Windows programs that offers object-oriented programming capabilities, allowing the programmer to draw the required screens and menus first, and then attach the necessary code to each item.

Volatile

Destined to be lost when the computer is turned off. Hard disk storage, for example, is non-volatile, because it remains available between uses of the computer; memory is volatile, because its contents are erased each time the computer is turned off.

WAN

Wide Area Network. Similar to a LAN, but extending over multiple buildings and/or sites.

Window

An area of the screen, usually enclosed by a border, that functions as a window (or view) into a portion of the program.

Windows

Microsoft Windows, a GUI for PCs.

Word wrap

The ability of an editor or word processor to automatically drop to the next line when the text on one line becomes too long. The word wrap feature (which is absent from most typewriters) prevents computer users from having to manually perform a carriage return at the end of each line.

X Window

A GUI standard that is common on Unix systems. X Window is only an interface standard, however; the actual look of the system can change. Motif is an example of an actual user interface for X Window.

xBASE

A standardized database management language, derived from the dBASE database management system. Many other DBMS programs also support xBASE.

Appendix C

Programming Languages and Compilers—A List of Vendors

t HIS appendix lists some of the more common vendors for C/C++, Pascal, BASIC, FORTRAN, COBOL, and several database languages. Each entry here includes a list of the different programming platforms supported by the product in question, along with pertinent contact information.

This is by no means a complete listing of every compiler or vendor currently available. Listings here do not mean that particular vendors are favored over others; there are probably other good compilers that have been overlooked here. In fact, for a real listing of the most important and well-known compilers, look at the most recent issue of one of the programming magazines listed in Appendix D.

Use this list as a starting point from which to select a compiler for your programming projects. Also, as you look through computer magazines, watch for these names under advertisements for programming tools; in this way you will find out which compilers have the best support (their names show up in the most advertisements for third-party tools).

When you are ready, call a few vendors to request their literature, and be sure ask for a demonstration disk! This will help you make your final decision.

C/C++

Packages:	Borland C++, Turbo C/C++
Platforms:	DOS, Windows and Windows NT, OS/2
Contacts:	800-336-6464, 408-438-8400
	Fax: 408-438-8696
	Borland International
	1800 Green Hills Road
	P.O. Box 660001
	Scotts Valley, CA 95067-0001

Packages:	EPC C and C++
Platforms:	Most major Unix implementations
Contacts:	408-438-1851
	Fax: 408-438-3510
	Edinburgh Portable Compilers
	20 Victor Square
	Scotts Valley, CA 95066

Package:	High C/C++
Platforms:	DOS, Windows and Windows NT, OS/2, AIX,
	Solaris, OSF, Unix
Contacts:	408-429-6382
	Fax: 408-429-9273
	MetaWare Incorporated
	2161 Delaware Avenue
	Santa Cruz, CA 95060-5706

Package:	IBM C Set++
Platform:	OS/2
Contacts:	800-3-IBM-OS2

Package:	Symantec C++ Standard and Professional Versions
Platforms:	DOS, Windows, and Windows NT
Contacts:	800-453-1077, 408-253-9600
	Symantec Corporation
	10201 Torre Avenue
	Cupertino, CA 95014

Packages:	TopSpeed C and C++
Platforms:	DOS, OS/2, Windows
Contacts:	800-354-5444
	Fax: 305-946-1650
	Clarion Software
	150 East Sample Road
	Pompano Beach, FL 33064

Package:	Visual C++ Standard and Professional Versions
Platforms:	Windows and Windows NT
Contacts:	800-227-4679, 206-882-8080
	Fax: 206-936-7329
	Microsoft Corporation
	One Microsoft Way
	Redmond, WA 98052-6399

Package:	WATCOM C/C++
Platforms:	DOS, Windows and Windows NT, OS/2
Contacts:	800-265-4555, 519-886-3700
	Fax: 519-747-4971
	WATCOM International Corp.
	415 Phillip Street
	Waterloo, Ontario Canada N2L 3X2

Pascal

Package: Pascal-E
Platforms: Most major Unix implementations
Contacts: 408-438-1851
Fax: 408-438-3510
Edinburgh Portable Compilers
20 Victor Square
Scotts Valley, CA 95066

Package: Pascal+
Platforms: DOS, Windows
Contacts: 800-624-7487, 805-496-7429
Fax: 805-496-5837
StonyBrook Software
187 E. Wilbur Rd., Suite 4
Thousand Oaks, CA 91360

Package: Professional Pascal
Platforms: DOS, Windows and Windows NT, OS/2, AIX,
Solaris, OSF, Unix
Contacts: 408-429-6382
Fax: 408-429-9273
MetaWare Incorporated
2161 Delaware Avenue
Santa Cruz, CA 95060-5706

Package: TopSpeed Pascal
Platforms: DOS, OS/2, Windows
Contacts: 800-354-5444
Fax: 305-946-1650
Clarion Software
150 East Sample Road
Pompano Beach, FL 33064

Packages: Turbo Pascal, Borland Pascal with Objects
Platforms: DOS, Windows
Contacts: 800-336-6464, 408-438-8400
Fax: 408-438-8696
Borland International
1800 Green Hills Road
P.O. Box 660001
Scotts Valley, CA 95067-0001

BASIC

Package:	CA-REALIZER
Platforms:	Windows, OS/2
Contacts:	800-225-5224
	Computer Associates International, Inc.
	One Computer Associates Plaza
	Islandia, NY 11788-7000

Package:	PowerBASIC
Platform:	DOS
Contacts:	800-245-6717, 408-730-9291
	Fax: 408-730-2107
	Spectra Publishing
	1030-D East Duane Ave.
	Sunnyvale, CA 94086

Package:	Visual BASIC Standard and Professional Versions
Platforms:	DOS, Windows
Contacts:	800-227-4679, 206-882-8080
	Fax: 206-936-7329
	Microsoft Corporation
	One Microsoft Way
	Redmond, WA 98052-6399

FORTRAN

Package:	Absoft F77
Platforms:	Windows NT, Macintosh, DOS, NeXTSTEP, Unix
Contacts:	313-853-0095
	Absoft
	2781 Bond St.
	Rochester Hills, MI 48309

Packages:	EPC FORTRAN 90 and FORTRAN 77
Platforms:	Most major Unix implementations
Contacts:	408-438-1851
	Fax: 408-438-3510
	Edinburgh Portable Compilers
	20 Victor Square
	Scotts Valley, CA 95066

Packages:	F77L, F77L EM/32, and Personal FORTRAN
Platform:	DOS
Contacts:	800-548-4778, 702-831-2500
	Fax: 702-831-8123
	Lahey Computer Systems Inc.
	P.O. Box 6091
	Incline Village, NV 89450

Package:	FORTRAN PowerStation
Platform:	Windows and Windows NT
Contacts:	800-227-4679, 206-882-8080
	Fax: 206-936-7329
	Microsoft Corporation
	One Microsoft Way
	Redmond, WA 98052-6399

Package:	NDP Fortran-90
Platforms:	DOS, OS/2, Unix, Solaris, Windows NT
Contacts:	508-746-7341
	Fax: 508-746-4678
	Microway
	Research Park
	Kingston, MA 02364

Package:	SVS C3 Fortran-77
Platforms:	Windows NT, Unix
Contacts:	415-572-8800
	Fax: 415-572-1685
	Silicon Valley Software
	1710 S. Amphlett Blvd., No. 100
	San Mateo, CA 94402

Package:	WATCOM FORTRAN-77/386
Platforms:	DOS, Windows, OS/2
Contacts:	800-265-4555, 519-886-3700
	Fax: 519-747-4971
	WATCOM International Corp.
	415 Phillip Street
	Waterloo, Ontario Canada N2L 3X2

COBOL

Package:	CA-Realia II Workbench
Platforms:	Windows, OS/2
Contacts:	800-225-5224
	Computer Associates International, Inc.
	One Computer Associates Plaza
	Islandia, NY 11788-7000

Package:	Micro Focus COBOL
Platforms:	DOS, Windows, OS/2
Contacts:	800-872-6265, 415-856-4161
	Micro Focus, Inc.
	2465 East Bayshore Road
	Palo Alto, CA 94303

Package:	Microsoft COBOL
Platform:	DOS
Contacts:	800-227-4679, 206-882-8080
	Fax: 206-936-7329
	Microsoft Corporation
	One Microsoft Way
	Redmond, WA 98052-6399

Database Languages

Packages:	Access, FoxPro, and SQL Server
Platforms:	DOS, Windows and Windows NT
Contacts:	800-227-4679, 206-882-8080
	Fax: 206-936-7329
	Microsoft Corporation
	One Microsoft Way
	Redmond, WA 98052-6399

Package:	Clarion Database Developer
Platform:	DOS
Contacts:	800-354-5444
	Fax: 305-946-1650
	Clarion Software
	150 East Sample Road
	Pompano Beach, FL 33064

Packages:	CA-Clipper, CA-dBFast
Platforms:	DOS, Windows
Contacts:	800-225-5224
	Computer Associates International, Inc.
	One Computer Associates Plaza
	Islandia, NY 11788-7000

Packages:	dBASE IV and dBASE Compiler, Paradox
Platforms:	DOS, Windows
Contacts:	800-336-6464, 408-438-8400
	Fax: 408-438-8696
	Borland International
	1800 Green Hills Road
	P.O. Box 660001
	Scotts Valley, CA 95067-0001

Package:	Ocelot SQL
Platforms:	DOS, Windows
Contacts:	403-421-4187
	Fax: 403-497-7342
	Ocelot Computer Services Inc.
	Suite 1104, Royal Trust Tower
	Edmonton, AB Canada, T5J 2Z2

Package:	ORACLE RDBMS
Platforms:	Windows, OS/2, Unix, and many others
Contacts:	800-345-DBMS, 415-506-7000
	Fax: 415-506-7200
	Oracle Corporation
	500 Oracle Parkway
	Redwood Shores, CA 94065

Package:	Sybase RDBMS
Platforms:	Windows NT, Unix, and many others
Contacts:	800-8-SYBASE, 510-596-3500
	Fax: 510-658-9441
	Sybase, Inc.
	6475 Christie Ave.
	Emeryville, CA 94608

Package:	WATCOM SQL
Platform:	Windows
Contacts:	800-265-4555, 519-886-3700
	Fax: 519-747-4971
	WATCOM International Corp.
	415 Phillip Street
	Waterloo, Ontario Canada N2L 3X2

Appendix D

Where to Find Out More

H E books listed in this appendix are recommended for helping you learn more about programming and software development; any one of them would also make a splendid reference volume even after you have read it the first time. The books are categorized here according to three broad topics:

◆ General software development

◆ Individual programming languages

◆ Programming for specific environments

A final list shows several good programming magazines.

Guides to General Software Development

Barker, Richard (with Cliff Longman). CASE*METHOD(tm) Series: *Entity Relationship Modelling, Tasks and Deliverables, Function and Process Modelling*. Addison-Wesley (Reading, MA). Although these books were written for users of the Oracle database, they have a very good introduction to CASE techniques, along with many useful examples.

Boddie, John. *Crunch Mode: Building Effective Systems on a Tight Budget*. Yourdon Press (Englewood Cliffs, NJ), 1987.

Campbell, Sally. *Microcomputer Software Design: How to Develop Complex Application Programs*. Prentice-Hall (Englewood Cliffs, NJ), 1984.

DeGrace, Peter, and Leslie Hulet Stahl. *Wicked Problems, Righteous Solutions: A Catalogue of Modern Software Engineering Paradigms*. Yourdon Press (Englewood Cliffs, NJ), 1990.

DeMarco, Tom, and Timothy Lister. *Peopleware: Productive Projects and Teams*. Dorset House Publishing (New York, NY), 1987.

Entsminger, Gary. *The Tao of Objects*. M&T Books (Redwood City, CA), 1990. Still one of the best introductions to object-oriented programming.

Glass, Robert L. *Software Conflict: Essays on the Art and Science of Software Engineering*. Yourdon Press (Englewood Cliffs, NJ), 1991.

James, Geoffrey. *The Tao of Programming*. InfoBooks (Santa Monica, CA). A small book of sayings and stories, some of which you have seen throughout this book.

Lammers, Susan. *Programmers at Work*. Microsoft Press (Redmond, WA), 1986.

von Mayrhauser, Anneliese. *Software Engineering: Methods and Management*. Academic Press (San Diego, CA), 1990.

Weinberg, Gerald M. *Understanding the Professional Programmer*. Dorset House Publishing (New York, NY), 1988.

Wirth, Niklaus. *Algorithms & Data Structures*. Prentice-Hall (Englewood Cliffs, NJ), 1986. A good introduction to algorithms, including sorting, searching, recursion, and more. The examples are in Modula-2, which is similar enough to Pascal that they can be used with few, if any, changes.

Yourdon, Edward. *Decline & Fall of the American Programmer*. Yourdon Press (Englewood Cliffs, NJ), 1992. One of the best overall introductions to the latest in software tools and methodologies, including CASE and OOP tools. Discusses how these advances might be used to improve the United States software industry.

Guides to Individual Programming Languages

Albrecht, Bob, Wenden Wiegand, and Dean Brown. *QuickBASIC Made Easy*. Osborne/McGraw-Hill (Berkeley, CA), 1989. A good coverage of the QuickBASIC compiler.

Christian, Kaare. *Borland C++ Techniques & Utilities*. Ziff-Davis Press (Emeryville, CA), 1993. Highly recommended for both DOS and Windows programming with the Borland C++ compiler. Covers many of the lesser known features of the Borland environment. Includes code on a disk.

Cornell, Gary. *The Visual Basic 3 for Windows Handbook*. Osborne/McGraw-Hill (Berkeley, CA), 1993. A good introduction to this new environment for Windows programming. Includes over 60 pages of answers to the most asked questions, directly from Microsoft.

Eckel, Bruce. *C++ Inside & Out*. Osborne/McGraw-Hill (Berkeley, CA), 1993. This is one of the standards you may wish to consider if you will be working with C++. Highly recommended.

Holzner, Steven. *Visual C++ Programming*. Brady Books (New York, NY), 1993. Includes a disk of samples.

Inman, Don, and Bob Albrecht. *QBASIC Made Easy*. Osborne/McGraw-Hill (Berkeley, CA), 1991. The most readable reference available on the QBASIC compiler, which is included with the most recent versions of DOS.

Jones, Edward. *The dBASE Language Reference*, Osborne/McGraw-Hill (Berkeley, CA), 1990. Good coverage of the language introduced with the dBASE product, including coverage of its use with Clipper, dBASE III and IV, dBXL, FoxBase and FoxPro, and Quicksilver.

Meyers, Scott. *Effective C++: 50 Specific Ways to Improve Your Programs and Designs*. Addison-Wesley (Reading, MA), 1992. Highly recommended.

O'Brien, Stephen, and Steve Nameroff. *Turbo Pascal 7: The Complete Reference*. Osborne/McGraw-Hill (Berkeley, CA), 1993. Great coverage of the Borland Pascal compilers, including Turbo Pascal, Turbo Pascal for Windows, and Borland Pascal with Objects.

Palmer, Scott D. *Programmer's Introduction to Turbo Pascal for Windows*. Sybex (Alameda, CA), 1992. A lot of good information for this compiler, including a disk of samples.

Pappas, Chris H., and William H. Murray III. *Borland C++ Handbook, Fourth Edition*. Osborne/McGraw-Hill (Berkeley, CA), 1994. Covers C++ and the use of Borland-specific development features.

Ribar, L. John. *C Disk Tutor*. Osborne/McGraw-Hill (Berkeley, CA), 1992. A hands-on introduction to C programming. Includes a disk with a C compiler and sample code.

Ribar, L. John. *FORTRAN Programming for Windows*. Osborne/McGraw-Hill (Berkeley, CA), 1993. A great introduction on how to bring existing FORTRAN code into the Windows environment.

Schildt, Herbert. *The Art of C: Elegant Programming Solutions*. Osborne/McGraw-Hill (Berkeley, CA), 1991. Includes a disk of useful routines and programs that can be combined with your own. Highly recommended.

Schildt, Herbert. *The Craft of C: Take Charge Programming*. Osborne/McGraw-Hill (Berkeley, CA), 1992. Highly recommended. Light, readable style; includes interviews with famous programmers. Very useful code. This book includes a disk.

Schildt, Herbert. *C: The Pocket Reference*. Osborne/McGraw-Hill (Berkeley, CA), 1991.

Schildt, Herbert. *C: The Complete Reference* and *C++: The Complete Reference*. Osborne/McGraw-Hill (Berkeley, CA), 1990 and 1991. Solid reference books with useful sample programs.

Schildt, Herbert. *Teach Yourself C* and *Teach Yourself C++*. Osborne/McGraw-Hill (Berkeley, CA), 1990 and 1992. Good overall introductions to these two languages.

Sessions, Roger. *Class Construction in C and C++*. Prentice-Hall (Englewood Cliffs, NJ), 1992. Fine introduction to object-oriented programming fundamentals using C and C++ examples.

Young, Michael J. *Mastering Microsoft Visual C++ Programming*. Sybex (Alameda, CA), 1993. Extremely good coverage of the Visual C++ compiler and tools. Includes a disk. Highly recommended.

Guides to Programming for Specific Environments

Dettman, Terry. *DOS Programmer's Reference, 2nd Edition*. Que Corporation (Carmel, IN), 1989.

Jourdain, Robert. *Programmer's Problem Solver for the IBM PC, XT & AT*. Brady Communications Company (New York, NY), 1986.

Murray, William H. III, and Chris H. Pappas. *Windows Programming: An Introduction,* Osborne/McGraw-Hill (Berkeley, CA), 1990. Basic introduction to programming for the Windows environment.

Porter, Anthony. *C++ Programming for Windows*. Osborne/McGraw-Hill (Berkeley, CA), 1993. Includes a disk with sample programs and reusable software objects.

Magazines

Circuit Cellar Ink: The Computer Applications Journal. 4 Park Street, Suite 20, Vernon, CT 06066. This magazine is especially good for those interested in controlling real-world devices with their programs.

The C Users Journal. 1601 West 23rd Street, Suite 200, Lawrence, KS 66046-2743. A good magazine for anyone interested in C programming. Includes articles for both beginning and advanced programmers. Also has a C bookstore and disk library.

Data Based Advisor. Box 469013, Escondido, CA 92046. Covers the database languages, including dBASE, Paradox, Clipper, FoxPro, client-server databases, and C programming.

Dr. Dobb's Journal (Software Tools for the Professional Programmer). P.O. Box 56188, Boulder, CO 80322-6188. A very good programmer's magazine, with lots of code in C, Pascal, and other languages.

Inside Series. The Cobb Group, 9420 Bunsen Parkway, Suite 300, Louisville, KY 40220. The Cobb Group publishes a wide range of newsletters, for most popular programming languages, applications, and environments. Contact them for your specific favorites. These newsletters have no advertising, and are filled with useful techniques and code examples.

Paradox Informant. 10519 E. Stockton Blvd., Suite 142, Elk Grove, CA 95624-9704. Dedicated to Paradox programmers.

PC Techniques. 7721 E. Gray Road, Suite 204, Scottsdale, AZ 85260-9747. A wonderful magazine for programmers using the IBM PC platform. Code in C and other languages, with lots of tips for programming the PC.

Software Development. P.O. Box 5032, Brentwood, TN 37024-5032. A good magazine for programmers of any language; many of the articles are dealing software development techniques and tools.

Visual Basic Programmer's Journal. P.O. Box 58872, Boulder, CO 80322-8872. A good magazine for those interested in Visual Basic programming.

Windows/DOS Developer's Journal. 1601 West 23rd Street, Suite 200. Lawrence, KS 66046-2743. Articles about programming for DOS and Windows operating systems; a good mixture of development techniques.

Windows NT Developer. P.O. Box 70167, Eugene, OR 97401-0110. A new magazine, dedicated to programming for the Windows NT operating system. Includes a monthly disk.

Windows Tech Journal. P.O. Box 70087, Eugene, OR 97401-9943. A very useful magazine for Windows programmers. Has an enjoyable writing style.

Index